T
F
S
E
V
W

PACIFIC OCEAN . . .

Coffee On The Wing Beam goes beyond the monotonous droning of engines to recall the excitement, luck, redeemable stupidity, brilliance and shenanigans of patrol aviation.

First flown in 1945, the P2V Neptune aircraft was the mainstay of the U.S. Navy's patrol and anti-submarine efforts through the late 1960s. In the hectic early days of the Korean War, Neptune crews were ordered to conduct strafing, rocket and bombing attacks on enemy troops in close air support of beleaguered U.S. and allied forces.

In Vietnam, Neptune crews were first tasked to conduct coastal patrols in Operation Market Time, but by 1967 two squadrons flying modified P2V aircraft had been formed to locate and interdict enemy truck traffic along the heavily-defended Ho Chi Minh Trail system. Yet, patrol aviation was anything but somber. There were many non-fatal goof ups and amusing shenanigans that crews could laugh about long after the fact.

Seen through the eyes of a young aviator, *Coffee On The Wing Beam* is a faithful and entertaining recollection of Neptune crews at work and at play.

Coffee On The Wing Beam

CAPT. Brian McGuiness USNR (Ret.)

KNIGHTS OF THE RED BRANCH PRESS
Clear Lake, Washington

Published by:
Knights of the Red Branch Press
P.O. Box 296
Clearlake, WA 98235-0296

Coffee On The Wing Beam

Copyright © 1997 by Capt. Brian McGuiness USNR (Ret.)

All rights reserved. No part of this publication may be reproduced or transmitted in any form or by any means, electronic or mechanical, photocopying, recording or any information and retrieval system without permission in writing from the publisher, except by a reviewer who may quote brief passages.

Library of Congress Catalog Card Number: 98-91665

ISBN 0-9665556-0-0

Printed in the United States of America

9 8 7 6 5 4 3 2

First printing

Title page art work by the author

DEDICATION

This book is dedicated to the tens of thousands of officers and men who flew in or maintained P2V Neptunes since the first prototype lifted off in late 1945.

Their hard work, diligence, stamina and courage played a substantive role in the post-World War II period, keeping track of the United States' maritime adversaries and ultimately helping to win the Cold War for democracy.

Though there were so many people involved in Neptune operations, very few personal accounts were written to describe the excitement, luck, redeemable stupidity, brilliance and shenanigans that made up the lives of patrol crews.

With sincere respect and a sense of my own good fortune, I chose to relate some of the highlights of my own years as a Neptune aviator to represent the thousands of additional stories that could be told.

ACKNOWLEDGEMENTS

I owe a hearty thanks to fellow Neptune pilots Bob McLaughlin and R.W. Webb for their encouragement to publish this recollection. I also wish to acknowledge my former squadron mate, Orin Humphries, who early on sent me valuable research material. My sincere appreciation also goes out to Bill Allen, a former Marine Corps aviator and Vietnam veteran; and Michael Barrett, an eminent journalist; for their help in critiquing the original manuscript.

CONTENTS

PROLOGUE.............................Pg. 1

Chapter 1:
   HOOKED BY *VICTORY AT SEA* ......Pg. 7
    * A problem of weight   10
    * First solo flight   13
    * Flying a Cadillac   15
    * Carrier qual   21

Chapter 2:
   FLYING BY COMMITTEE ....Pg. 30
    * The 'Stoof'   31
    * Carrier, commission and wings 33
    * Where's Whidbey Island?   35
    * The ferocious turtle   38
    * To the breakwater for dinner   47
    * Escape, evasion and POW camp   52
    * A small, big mistake   56
    * Relief tube was no relief   65

Chapter 3:
   VIETNAM ....Pg. 69
    * Operation Market Time   74
    * 'Chieu Hoi' Psy Ops   80
    * 'Who shit all over my airplane' 84
    * Flying 'In country'   91
    * Island-hopping home   94

Chapter 4:
   BOMBS AWAY, AND OTHER STUFF... Pg. 99
    * Kelly's Bombaydears   102
    * 'I got the quals'   105
    * Sniff around like a beagle   111
    * Smile, look at the birdie   112
    * The blood-red ocean   114
    * How low did you go?   116

Chapter 5:
   VIETNAM, THE TEMPO INCREASES...Pg. 119
    * Sunrise zombies   120
    * Skyscraper out of the darkness 122
    * Operating in the Tonkin Gulf 128
    * Sister squadron loses aircraft 130
    * Operation 'San Magoo'   133
    * Boarding sampans   136

Chapter 6:
    NORTH KOREANS SEIZE *PUEBLO*.....Pg. 142
       * Loaded for bear   146
       * Armed and dangerous   148
       * The sealed manila envelopes   151

Chapter 7:
    GUN-RUNNING TRAWLERS ....Pg. 154
       * Trawler turns tail   154
       * Four trawlers make a run   157

Chapter 8:
    P2V SPECIAL OPS IN VIETNAM......Pg. 164
       * VO-67: The green machines   165
       * VAH-21: Trail interdiction   171
       * The Army's Crazy Cats   174

Chapter 9:
    LOW ALTITUDE AND HIGH JINKS....Pg. 176
       * Wrestling with Saint Elmo   177
       * Bow pilot: 'I've got it'   184
       * 'Aircraft on our tail'   187
       * Moon under Honolulu   190

Chapter 10:
    NEPTUNE REIGNS ....Pg. 193
       * Eight Neptune variants   193
       * Concept and prototypes   193
       * P2V-1   195
       * P2V-2   196
       * P2V-3   197
       * P2V-4 (P-2D)   200
       * P2V-5 (P-2E)   201
       * P2V-6 (P-2F)   205
       * P2V-7 (P-2H)   207
       * P-2J   210

Bibliography   211

Book order form   214

Illustrations:
       T-28 Trojan basic trainer   17
       SP-2H fuselage interior   46
       Market Time patrol area map   79
       Chieu Hoi Psy Ops leaflet   81, 82
       SP-2H rocket pattern   107
       Pueblo operational area map   147

AUTHOR'S NOTE

Though I thoroughly enjoyed jotting down my recollections of flying the P2V Neptune for this publication, recalling events that occurred over 30 years ago with great accuracy was a daunting exercise. I took great care during the process to verify all the individual stories that make up the book against the many publications and newspapers of the period that documented the Navy's participation in the Korean and Vietnam wars, the seizure of the USS *Pueblo*, and the many less-dramatic events of the Cold War.

As painstakingly as I tried to be in confirming each story, it was an impossible task. Thus, to ensure total accuracy in any future printing, I would welcome hearing from any reader who might like to share information he has on any of the events described in *Coffee On The Wing Beam*. A note to the publisher's address would be most welcomed.

To protect the privacy of two individuals highlighted in chapters four and nine, I have taken the liberty of changing their names.

Coffee On The
Wing Beam

PROLOGUE

Oh, to be alive! It gives me pause to reminisce with a considerable amount of amazement and a quiet sense of good fortune on all my years of flying and the numerous times my crews and I came so close to buying the farm.

Thirty years ago, as a young Navy pilot flying in Vietnam, I saw the missions as usually exciting but frequently dangerous. With a little different perspective today, I now see the assignments were more often in the hands of fate: What possessed us on one particularly-dark night to turn on our searchlight at just the right moment to avoid flying into the side of a ship? Why did the crew of an apparently doomed North Vietnamese gun-running trawler choose not to fire their 12.7-mm antiaircraft deck gun at us when we flew by them at point-blank range?

With such fateful questions to ponder, I often shake my head and smile in recalling the hair-raising, brilliant, lucky, and just plain stupid things we did to accomplish our missions.

But to share all those stories with you, I have to take you back to the early 1950s to an Archie Bunker-type home in New York City to a scrawny, impressionable kid sitting in front of a new Emerson black and white television set being totally mesmerized by the awesome sights and triumphant symphonic sounds of the *Victory at Sea* series. I watched it religiously for months, both fighting off my older sister and delaying the delivery of my newspaper route, on occasion, so that I wouldn't miss an episode.

I was hooked at that early age and knew, in great deference to my exceedingly gruff active-duty master sergeant grandfather, that I wanted someday to be a Navy flyboy. Even though the formidable "Sarge" had won World War I, World War II and the Korean Conflict single-handedly for the U.S. Army, there just could not be any story he told that compared with the excitement of naval aviation; being up there in the blue, skirting the blinding-white edges of billowing-gray clouds in an aircraft with the canopy drawn back, looking for danger, or trying to find that small postage stamp in the sea they called an aircraft carrier.

Well, as it turned out, I had the luck and perseverance to become a naval aviator by twenty-two years of age, and that open cockpit of my fantasies quickly came true in the training command. It was as exciting as I thought it was going to be in the T-28 "Trojan" aircraft—which looked somewhat like a World War II

Hellcat—as I made my first arrested landings on the carrier *Lexington*.

But, alas, my dreams of becoming a carrier pilot did not fit the needs of the U.S. Navy. Instead of hooking cables on the angled decks of carriers, I was assigned to patrol aviation where my landings would be alternately on concrete or the steel runway matting of some airfields in Vietnam.

My heart had been set on flying carrier attack or fighter aircraft, but not necessarily jets. The prop-driven A-1 Skyraider or "Spad" attack aircraft was still in service at the time and appealed to me the most, but the Navy was quickly transitioning those squadrons to jets as the A-6 Intruders came on line. Nevertheless, nearing the completion of the advanced training command, I applied on my dream sheet to fly prop attack. In retrospect, the fact that I am still reminiscing today, well aware of the many close calls I witnessed in my safer fleet aircraft, is probably a consequence of not getting exactly what I wanted.

About a week before I was to begin training in my new patrol assignment, I received a history lesson from the lips of an incredibly knowledgeable sweetheart who was a happy hour regular at an officer's club in California. My head, admittedly, was still full of Wildcats, Hellcats, Trojans and Skyraiders when my bar stool tutor informed me that the most famous P2V Neptune patrol aircraft in flying history had been the "Truculent Turtle." Up to that time, I had limited knowledge of the aircraft, and I only took some small comfort later that evening when I found the meaning of truculent in my well-worn college dictionary to be "ferocious, savage or cruel." I certainly got a chuckle about that one; I was getting ready to train in a ferocious turtle.

Within days of completing the P2V ground school, I was in the cockpit of the vintage World War II-designed aircraft flying out of the Naval Air Station at North Island in San Diego. A member of the training crew described the aircraft as "two-turn' in and two-burn'in," owing to the unusual configuration of two huge piston and two pure jet engines that the "Hotel" model had on its 101-foot-long wing span. I also came to find out the P2V had long legs; that is to say, it stayed in the air a long time, twelve hours on occasion. Thus, the often-heard saying about patrol aviation, "Hours and hours of boredom, punctuated by moments of sheer terror," was fairly accurate. At the least, we always needed to be on our toes for those numerous unscheduled moments of sheer terror.

Coffee kept us going. It was an essential part of flying for nine to twelve hours "per hop," low and slow over the waterways of the world. All too often, to the chagrin of many operational commanders, rigid takeoff times for missions were busted when coffee grounds did not arrive at the aircraft in a timely manner from the base galley. It was that important to the crews.

Not only were the flights long, but considering crew members who stayed out celebrating into the early hours, the short fitful periods of sleep, the long briefs and preflights, we all needed something more than just lift to keep us in the air. Coffee gave us that edge.

The designers of the P2V Neptune in the mid-1940s most assuredly did not have coffee on their minds when they configured the strong, prominent wing box or beam right through the middle of the fuselage. There was just enough space left for crew members to crawl over the long, curved beam on their hands and knees.

Yet, as essential as it was, the thirty-cup coffee pot was nevertheless designed to be plugged in the back of the aircraft where only three crew members were stationed. All the remaining eight crew members were forward of the wing beam. Thus, when there was a call for coffee from the bow observer, cockpit or flight deck, a steaming cup had to be carefully placed on top of the wing beam for pickup. This required a lot of communications and coordination over the aircraft's internal communications system.

"Coffee on the wing beam" was an often-repeated, if not the most repeated, utterance that came over the crew's headsets in the P2V. If you can imagine in the typical turbulent environment of low-altitude flight, an inviting cup of hot brew waiting to be picked up from the crown of a vibrating wing beam would not stay there for very long.

Unless a crewman was in the middle of one of those moments of sheer terror, "Coffee on the wing beam" elicited a quick response from the crewman who needed the liquid jolt.

Chapter 1

HOOKED BY *VICTORY AT SEA*

I was a child of World War II and its retrospective victory celebrations. All the kids like me growing up in the late 1940s and early 1950s were barraged by an unending series of "we won the war" movies and documentaries.

In the New York City Borough of Queens where I was raised, our typical weekends started out by getting together with our gangs—not the same connotation as today—to head down to one of two small movie theaters, both within a short walking distance. The theater managers had us hooked with contests, kiddie prizes, oodles of cartoons and two full-length feature films, all for only twenty-five cents. We looked forward to Saturday mornings because we knew we would thoroughly enjoy ourselves wherever we decided to go.

My choice of which theater to attend was based on the films. For whatever reason, I was more oriented to action movies, not necessarily the blood-and-gore genre, but with actors whose characters would do the right thing. When I was growing up, most of the movie plots stressed high moral themes. I can still recall how impressionable I was coming out of a theater one early afternoon, squinting in the bright sunlight but emotionally reliving the Knights of the Round Table and their deeds, running home as if I was a knight on an intrepid horse, jousting with black, creosoted telephone poles along the way.

Moreover, after seeing one particular jungle war movie, I was motivated to sit quietly and still in my backyard just to see if I had the stamina and discipline to surprise the birds that landed to feed at my mother's spread of sunflower seeds and cracked corn. My intent was not to harm the birds—I knew better than that! I just wanted to emulate the American war heros in the movie, to see if I had what it took to be as disciplined.

When I was about seven years old, the new medium of television was being mass-produced enough for my family to afford a small set. My uncle, a returning U. S. Army veteran of the South Pacific, learned electronics in the military and got a job after his discharge at one of the early television production lines in New Jersey. As a result of his employee discount, all of his brothers living nearby were literally the first ones on their blocks to get TV sets. By 1953, television was giving movie theaters a run for their money, offering cartoons and kids' shows on Saturday mornings. At this same time, television was also the medium chosen to give adults a dramatic retrospective look and stirring symphonic interpretation of the past war through the eyes of naval personnel. I can only analyze now that I must have been at the peak of my impressionable years when I saw my first episode of *Victory At Sea*. I was captivated by the series, but especially by the scenes that showed Navy pilots and aircraft carriers.

Having a maternal grandfather who was an ancient Army master sergeant "Retread" for serving in both World Wars I and II, and who had just returned from fighting in Korea to continue his service in the states, there was no doubt that one day I would serve in the military. Even at that early age I thought of it as an obligation to fulfill, just like Grandpa. The danger was not a consideration for someone so young, but from the few stories the "Sarge" would tell, particularly the time he admitted letting loose in his combat fatigues when incoming shells landed close, it became clear to me with each telecast of the sights and electrifying sounds of the Richard Rogers' score that I did not want to join the Army.

My grandfather was extremely proud of being a combat infantryman, but I could not favorably compare his exploits with the billowing and blue environment of a carrier pilot, flying high, looking for enemy aircraft or protecting the ships below on the sea.

I recall one early Sunday morning in the winter, I was so pumped up after watching a *Victory At Sea* episode that I literally pulled my iron monster of a bicycle into the air many times from sidewalk curbs to the snow-filled streets on my newspaper route. I was simulating the exact moment when a Navy pilot had to lift his plane off the deck of a fast-moving aircraft carrier or sink to the waves below.

A problem of weight

Though of medium height, I was always a scrawny kid. This carried over into being a young adult with a year of college and a yearning to join the Naval Reserve and begin accumulating longevity. While I was continuing college, I joined the reserves as an enlisted man at nineteen. I had every intention of completing four years for a degree before applying for the Navy's Aviation Officer Candidate (AOC) flight program, but I soon became focused and excited about a cadet flight program that allowed qualified young men to begin pilot training after only two years of college credit.

Being curious as to how I would do, I took the Naval Aviation Cadet (NAVCAD) tests and passed them all, except one little aspect of the medical exam—I was too skinny. As odd as this sounds today, the examining doctor at that time told me I would have several opportunities while completing my second year of college to put on five pounds to meet the minimum weight requirement of the flight program. It must have been hilarious for my friends to see me so often chomping down on bananas and ice cream and slurping milk shakes; yet, after seven months I had gained only four pounds. My body really suffered to put on that last pound; it was not used to cramming down all those calories, but I passed my last physical exam right on the minimum weight mark.

Things occurred rapidly after that exam with quick acceptance into the NAVCAD program and a class assignment date in September 1964. I kept up my weight regimen to be on the safe side, but all of that was for naught in respect to the arduous physical exercising that began in Pensacola, Florida, within hours of walking through the door at preflight school. Before we were even issued uniforms and utilities the next afternoon, the Marine drill sergeants had us cadets up at 5:30 A.M. doing pushups, situps and running in the same suits we arrived in the day before. I didn't have a way to tell for sure, but I think in the hot Florida sun I lost my five hard-earned pounds in the first week of training.

Preflight school was four months of taking orders, standing at attention, jumping, swimming, marching, running, crawling, training to survive, intensive studying, and covering up the wild dreams we had at night about beautiful women.

As much as I tried to avoid trouble and keep from getting military demerits—which we had to march off each week—I could not avoid them. Once, while I was alertly approaching the rear entrance to a barracks, one of our more-uptight drill sergeants came busting out the door. I immediately and smartly stepped to the side of the concrete pathway with the intention of standing at attention and giving him the proper military courtesy: "By your leave, sergeant." Instead, I stepped into a small hole hidden in the grass and nearly toppled over. Needless to say, I was so flustered I failed to greet the sergeant at all. As I regained my stance, the gruff sergeant was in my face and bellowing, "What's your next move, ex lax?" Before I could respond, he was quick to add, "Put yourself on report, mister," which cost me another hour of disciplinary marching in front of my battalion barracks.

Months later, after passing all the academic, military and physical fitness tests, we were no longer raw recruits but cadet officers who now would command the newly arriving cadet classes for two weeks. At our graduation from preflight school, to the disbelief of the ancient but distinguished retired admiral who was handing out diplomas, I won the physical fitness award by having the highest grades out of my class of sixty-five cadets. "I truly commend you; but how did you do it, you're so thin?" the admiral asked inquisitively. So much for five pounds, I was thinking to myself.

First solo flight

Primary flight training at Saufley Field, Florida, just north of Pensacola, was our next hurdle as cadets. On the road to becoming a naval aviator, primary training would see us through our first solo flights and give us a taste of aerobatics.

Refreshingly, the new regimen was slightly less military and more oriented to ground school study and syllabus hops in the prop-driven T-34 Mentor. We studied advanced aerodynamics, engineering, cockpit procedures and safety precautions for two weeks before being assigned our first flight in Training Squadron One. Thereafter, we spent six weeks of split workdays between ground school and the flight line to correlate the information we had learned in the morning by flying in the afternoon.

In this squadron we felt the beginnings of an "esprit de corps" develop when we attained a certain flying milestone and were recognized for it by those in command at weekend parties. Halfway through the twelfth flight with an instructor, if he felt a student had mastered everything and was ready to fly solo, he directed the fledgling to an outlying field (OLF), where he got out of the back seat of the aircraft and gave the student a thumbs up to proceed with one solo takeoff and landing. Having an instructor with a sense of humor on my solo-check flight, he shouted over the noise of the idling engine, "And don't forget to pick me up before you fly back to Saufley."

I recall my first solo-check flight—as short as it was—like the final scenes from the movie classic, *Waldo Pepper*, even with the music. It was exhilarating. I was alone in an open cockpit, flying in the clouds—but woke from this dream just in time to land the T-34 safely. I had been gone only three minutes, taking off and circling the field just once, to land and pick up my instructor.

The very next day, I was scheduled for my first solo flight. What a thrill, and what dread. There wasn't going to be anyone there to bail me out if I screwed up. Nevertheless, the only syllabus requirements I can remember were to come back in 1.3 hours, conduct multiple touch-and-go landings at a designated OLF and remain within safety and Federal Aviation Administration flight regulations. After completing five landings at a field west of Saufley, I took off scouting the Florida-Alabama border area until I spied hundreds of World War II Liberty ships at anchor in the northern reaches of Mobile Bay. I never asked the other cadets what they did on their first solo flights, but I cleared the area below me visually for other aircraft and commenced several power-back shallow dive-bombing runs on the moored ships, imagining the heroic actions of the Douglas Dauntless divebomber pilots at the decisive Battle of Midway—before reality and the time to begin the flight back was upon me. I was only too happy later that week to participate in the tradition of having my black uniform tie cut off by my instructor pilot at a squadron happy hour to signify the successful completion of my first solo flight.

After the solo phase, our training intensified as we were focused on precision and proficiency flying. In only eleven short flights—two with instructors—we learned the acrobatic loop, full Cuban eight, the wingover, barrel roll, and how to recover and get out of a dangerous spin. Completion of this stage was a real morale booster that gave us the confidence to handle an aircraft alone in good weather.

Flying a Cadillac

The next stage of training was the basic prop syllabus. This required us to move to NAS Whiting Field in Milton, Florida, not very far from Pensacola. The training in two variants of the T-28 Trojan aircraft was hard work but a real kick in the pants. I had some rough spots in the six months it took to complete this stage culminating in carrier landings, but looking back, I recall this as the most satisfying flying in my career. Like my fantasies of *Victory At Sea*, this is where I was more often alone, strapped inside a powerful aircraft that was wonderful to fly.

This stage of training was a tremendous step for all of us fledgling aviators. Coming out of training in the T-34, the T-28 was much heavier, had much more power, climbed and cruised higher and faster, and could perform aerobatics that the previous aircraft could not. In fact, the T-28 "Bravo" model we flew in this stage had a top speed of nearly 300 knots, which made it comparable in performance to many early World War II fighters. As one instructor remarked, "It's like driving a Cadillac after you've been driving a Volkswagen."

At Whiting Field our training was split between Training Squadrons Two and Three. The first unit included quite a lot of ground school before getting to the flight line to accomplish eight dual instruction flights and one solo. We were in awe of this powerful aircraft as we were taught to takeoff and land, climb and descend and how to deal with high- and low-altitude emergencies. Later on, we learned precision-landing procedures and how to perform wingover, loop, barrel roll, half Cuban eight and Immelman aerobatic maneuvers. Basic instrument flying was next, which was somewhat intimidating. We were placed in the back seat of the tandem T-28 and flew it from beneath a canvas hood that blocked out all references to the ground. No matter what physical forces we felt our bodies were telling us, we learned to rely strictly upon the aircraft instruments as the true depiction of the aircraft's attitude, altitude and speed.

Another formidable stage for student pilots was night flying. Without the confidence gained to rely upon the aircraft's flight instruments, our minds could easily play visual tricks on us as the stars often blended into the landscape of sparsely lighted terrain on black, moonless nights. Up or down, it could all look the same.

T-28 Trojan basic trainer

At Training Squadron Three, basic instrument flying was refined and radio navigation was introduced to us in the venerable Link Trainer. The trainer was an operator monitored box-shaped, moving caricature of an aircraft with stubby wings. There was just enough room for the student to sit enclosed in a simulated cockpit with instruments, the same as those in an actual aircraft. In the trainer, we could practice instrument flying and simulated instrument approaches to various airfields, all without ever leaving the ground.

After using what we learned from this trainer on actual flights, we were assigned to a formation-flying training unit. Here we were taught two-plane and four-plane section flying. The wild two-plane "tail chase" practice, I recall, was the most fun and was the syllabus hop that came as close to a dogfight as anything I ever again experienced. The lead aircraft would bank sharply to the left and descend 500 feet while making a 90-degree compass heading change. Then it would immediately bank to the right and begin climbing back to the original altitude and heading. The second aircraft would chase the first, using power, as necessary, to remain on its tail, simulating and maintaining a continuous, potential shoot-down position.

The formation-flying stage was also the first time my peers and I came face to face with our own mortality. Since we must have had an excess of bravado to be in the flight program anyway, I can recall the many times a gaggle of student pilots would toast each other at a bar or club with, "Stall, spin, crash, burn, die." Of course, we weren't singing about ourselves, that wouldn't happen to us; we were all too young and full of vinegar. The reality of that chant, however, came true early one afternoon in mid-1965 when flight operations were abruptly suspended because of a search for two student aviators who were overdue from separate day-solo flights. All available squadron instructors were ordered into the air to join the regular Sea, Air Rescue (SAR) units operating from Whiting Field and nearby Pensacola. In the mostly swampy area of the western Florida Panhandle, we were told it would be difficult to locate any missing aircraft unless a crash started a fire, was witnessed, or there was a crash survivor who was actively seeking to be rescued. Emergency locator transmitters (ELTs) were not in use in the mid-1960s, so finding survivors or crash sites would be tough.

The squadron's operations office directed the rescuers to the area it believed the two were operating within, but darkness caused a halt to the effort. When the names of the missing were announced, I realized I had known one of the students personally, a Marine cadet who had been in a class ahead of me at preflight school. Though I had lost track of him in the months prior to this presumed accident, it still was sobering to be called into our squadron ready room late the next morning for a series of post-accident safety lectures. At that meeting, we heard that two crash sites had been found just after daybreak in swampy brush land. Two large water-filled impact craters more than one mile apart indicated both aircraft hit the earth in a near vertical entry. Helicopters had been rushed to both scenes for extensive ground searches, but neither site produced a survivor who would have been eager to light a flare and be rescued—just like all of us had been trained to do.

Since both pilots had been lost, speculation loomed at the time that the two aircraft had been involved in a midair collision. Damage must have been extensive to both aircraft since neither pilot apparently had the opportunity to bail out of his wreck.

In military aviation, the talk of death is often clouded in euphemisms to cushion the pain or loss. In that context and with no disrespect, my former cadet friend and the other student had "bought the farm" in their passing.

A little over a year after arriving at preflight school, I finished the instrument and formation flying in the T-28. The highlight of this final training was a five-plane formation navigation flight from Whiting Field to Memphis, Tennessee, using only a terrain map and visual aids. A bend in a river, a highway intersection, a radio tower, the shape and size of a lake, all became fixed landmarks that gave our aircraft formation new compass headings over the 360 miles to Memphis. Yet, when we got back to our base late the next day, we had little time to savor our accomplishment or mourn our recent losses, for we had our greatest challenge immediately before us: Carrier qualification, or as they would say in the student's vernacular of the time, "We were going to hit the boat."

Carrier qual

Though a non-lethal foible cost me a bottle of vodka, my carrier qualification in the T-28 was otherwise totally satisfying. Only a few events in my additional nineteen years of military flying were as personally fulfilling. All of the flight skills we had learned so far, all of the confidence we had acquired, and all of the fantasies that inspired me personally to pursue naval aviation came together in this one syllabus.

Unlike all the previous course work which involved so many different subjects and flight experiences, carrier qualification was incredibly focused and took less than four weeks to complete. For the first time in all our training, we were completely absorbed by the exacting procedures required for carrier operations, and we loved every minute of it. We also felt we were being treated differently by our ground and flight instructors, who must have taken distinct satisfaction in seeing their fledglings accomplish the one feat that set all naval aviators apart from their contemporaries in the other services. To say I was thrilled at this point in my life is an understatement. At just twenty-one years of age, I was about to embark on what I had always dreamed of, shades of *Victory At Sea*, visions of an open cockpit aircraft turning base to a straight-in approach to a carrier deck.

In mid-October 1965, I moved my belongings back to Pensacola and Saufley Field where Training Squadron Five would hone the skills of my classmates and me to bring a T-28 aboard the venerable World War II carrier, USS *Lexington*. The T-28 "Charlie" model, a variant of the Trojan with a retractable tailhook, was heavier than the aircraft we were used to flying, but the extra weight did not appreciably affect the flight characteristics.

After just two days of ground school, we were scheduled for three flights with instructors to teach us the unusual slow flight carrier approach configuration. All of our remaining flights in this syllabus were solo. As I remember, the slow flight airspeed for a proper carrier approach was just 10 to 12 knots above full stall, and, at first, the nose-high attitude of the aircraft was a bit uncomfortable. If you consider sitting on a chair being tipped back to where it begins to feel unbalanced, this is how the T-28C felt when set up in a nose-high attitude for a carrier landing.

As our training had taught us, we had to rely upon our instruments and put our natural human tendencies aside. In just a few rides we became proficient in this new flight experience and were able to control the descent on glide path strictly with aircraft attitude and engine power.

A new dimension to flying the T-28C to a carrier landing was the open canopy. Though all the other operations were performed with a closed canopy, it was necessary as a safety precaution for the T-28 canopy to be open while making the near-to-stall carrier approach. With no explosive release for the canopy, a pilot wouldn't be able to extricate himself from the cockpit if he stalled and crashed into the sea. An open cockpit was a thrill, but the loud rush of air made it nearly impossible for me to hear radio transmissions.

Once we were comfortable flying the nose-high carrier configuration of the T-28C, we began to make practice precision approaches to runways setup with optical landing systems. These mirror and illuminated Fresnel lens systems, the same as installed on every U.S. carrier, projected a beam of light that provided an optimum glide angle for a pilot in an approaching aircraft to visually follow to the deck. The angle of the beam would be determined by the carrier's Landing Signal Officer (LSO) based upon his experience in changing weather conditions, and the pitching of the deck in rough seas. A pilot banking his aircraft to line up with the carrier's angled landing deck would begin to see the beam and fly to align it with a row of horizontal lights.

When the beam, or "meatball," was aligned on the same plane as the horizontal lights, the aircraft was on the proper glide path. When the meatball was higher or lower than the horizontal reference lights, the aircraft was respectively higher or lower than the optimum glide path to the carrier's aft deck where four steel cables were in wait to capture a tailhook.

The day of our carrier qual on the *Lexington* dawned foggy. We had driven west of Pensacola to Barin Field to arrive before the sun was due to rise. We were all anxious, which increased as we sat in our cramped ready room waiting for the fog to clear. I was starting to relax by focusing on the many operating and emergency procedures for the flight, when someone called my name. Our class instructor, who would follow our flight of five out but stay at altitude to monitor our performance, had chosen me to lead the gaggle out. I don't think anyone in my flight had ever considered who might have to go first, so to this day I don't know whether the instructor's choice was an honor or a misgiving. Nonetheless, I had been an enthusiastic student and performed well in the training phase.. .but all that admittedly wasn't "the boat."

Just about the time we were getting ready to hang it up for the day, our instructor came busting through the door to announce the weather had cleared in the northern Gulf of Mexico and the *Lexington* was ready to receive our approaches and landings. Very quickly, we manned our aircraft, took off and joined up in a right echelon formation flight to follow the compass headings the instructor radioed to us from his higher, trailing position.

When we first saw the *Lexington* steaming in the gulf, we were flying at 3,000 feet. Even at that low altitude, the "Lex" looked small— not quite like a postage stamp—but small. Our instructor gave us the go-ahead to descend into the landing pattern. I took the flight over the carrier at 1,000 feet paralleling the ship's course and broke off to the left to begin my descent downwind in the opposite direction. After my landing gear, flaps, and speed brake came down, the other aircraft broke off and followed me downwind at appropriate intervals.

Abeam the stern of the carrier, I began a lefthand turn to align my nose-high aircraft with the landing deck and to radio the carrier that I had caught sight of the "meatball." The plan was for each aircraft to do two touch-and-go and six arrested landings.

My first approach to a touch-and-go with tailhook up was going smoothly, almost too smoothly—something was not quite right—but I couldn't figure it out in the seconds before I saw a flashing engine-chop light signal from the LSO on board. I immediately chopped my throttle, hit the angled deck solidly on the center line, and then rammed my throttle forward again for full power as the T-28C jumped back into the air.

God that felt good. With that feeling of bliss, I edged the stick a little to the right to parallel the course of the carrier and climbed back up to the landing-pattern altitude. My bliss was short-lived as a clearly audible LSO on the Lex's deck called my aircraft side number insisting that I "open" my canopy for the next touch-and-go and the duration of the arrested landings.

That's what was wrong. My canopy had been closed! I could hear the radio traffic clearly. Time for a little anxiety.

Because of that little foible, my mind's inner voice was quite clear, even though it was lower than a whisper: "He who screws up a carrier approach without creating chaos or worse owes the ship's LSO a bottle of his choice for spoiling his day." Thus, after a talk with the LSO on a radio telephone after I got back, I was happy but embarrassed to donate a bottle of vodka for his future enjoyment.

As fate would grant me for the rest of the flight, I opened my canopy, avoided any more bottles owed, and literally could not fathom one more radio transmission until my canopy was closed at the end of the carrier-landing exercise.

Following the second touch-and-go, I set up for an arrested landing. Now with the tailhook down, I called sight of the meatball and proceeded inbound on the glide path at 82 knots. Considering the carrier was cruising at 30 knots, my aircraft received the chop signal close in and made contact with the steel deck at a relative speed of only 52 knots. The hook caught the wire about the same time I was advancing the throttle. This was the procedure in case the aircraft failed to catch a wire—it would have full engine power already applied to successfully takeoff again.

The jolt to a complete stop on the deck was the signal to reduce engine power to idle and then look to the right for directions from the deck handling officer. My T-28C was slowly pulled backwards for a short distance to disengage the tailhook.

Then the hook and speed brake were retracted. The deck officer had me taxi forward about one hundred feet to prepare for a free deck launch, straight ahead off the ship's bow ramp.

Today, all aircraft except helicopters and jump jets are catapulted from carrier decks. The T-28C was one of only a few naval aircraft in the 1960s that still could accomplish a carrier takeoff using its own power. Now spotted forward of the angled deck where another T-28 was being arrested to a full-stop landing, the launch officer gave me the familiar twirling-fingers engine power signal. My throttle was advanced to full power, while the brakes were held hard. Only after the officer pointed his fingers forward to the bow ramp were the brakes released and the T-28C began its run. The incredibly-slow acceleration surprised me, but this was quite logical considering the reality of an invisible 30-knot wind slowing the T-28's progress down the deck.

The airspeed indicator was just beginning to register as the T-28C neared the bow, but this was of lesser concern than the necessity to raise the nose wheel off the deck to a takeoff attitude before the end of the ramp or risk drifting down into the sea just in front of the carrier's crushing bow. I had practiced this many times as a newspaper boy, jumping curbs with my bicycle—and it worked for me now.

My subsequent arrested landings and one waveoff on short final because of a fouled deck—another aircraft still being disconnected from the wires—went well, and when it was all over, I formed up with my classmates, now last in our formation for the flight back to our field. This whirlwind rite of passage for five of us fledgling naval aviators took less than one-and-a-half hours to complete, from takeoff to return to Barin Field.

For me, this was the most exciting time in my Navy flying career. Even the carrier qual in the twin-engine S-2 Tracker five months later paled in comparison. This flight had been truly unique. I had been all alone in the T-28 and with all other things being equal was solely responsible for the success or failure of my carrier qualification.

My next assignment, the advanced training command, would eventually lead to Navy wings of gold. Four months of training lay ahead in Corpus Christi, Texas, on all aspects of multi-engine and multi-piloted aviation operations and navigation. However, unlike the fourteen months of previous training that stressed individual responsibility and attainment, a totally new concept was stressed that would play a key role in all my future years in naval aviation: Flying by Committee.

Chapter 2

FLYING BY COMMITTEE

Teamwork was the most dramatic change we learned in the advanced training command. In all of our previous pilot evaluations, the emphasis had been solely on individual achievement. Now at Corpus Christi, Texas, our focus was shifted to a new concept that stressed crew teamwork, coordination and reliance.

We never had a formal class on the subject, so teamwork was learned intuitively and through lots of trial and error. It was a continuing process which occurred as often as new crew members were assigned to fly with us.

Before advanced training, we had been acknowledged for our own initiative, aggressiveness, knowledge and ability. Now we had to step back and see ourselves as part of a team, like a wheel that is made up of many individual cogs. True to form, someone in our class came up with a new expression for this radical departure from our former individuality, to convey both our approval of and sometimes frustration with the teamwork concept. Another euphemism, he called it "flying by committee."

The Navy's insistence upon standardized training and certification for each flight position was the key to teamwork when it shined. Flying by committee seemed only to falter when an individual's subjective "attitude" was not up to the same level as his ability. Thankfully, the committee system worked more often than not in crews that knew their jobs, were willing to work hard, were motivated and enthusiastic, and showed it all by example. Good teamwork was infectious.

In looking back, it was the teamwork and the outstanding abilities of the overwhelming number of people I had the honor and pleasure to serve with that made fateful decisions based on their intuition and experience just at the right times for all of us to avoid "buying the farm."

The 'Stoof'

I arrived at Corpus Christi in late November 1965 and was assigned to VT-31 for seventeen weeks of instruction and flight familiarization in the S-2A Tracker aircraft. This was my first introduction to a multi-engine aircraft that required the coordination of two pilots to fly. After two weeks of ground school covering the S-2's unique engineering and flight performance, safety and survival training, and advanced meteorology, we split our syllabus time between short introductory flights and cockpit simulators on the ground.

The Tracker, or "Stoof" as it was more affectionately called, was truly an interesting aircraft. Its design made it look stubby, with a wing span twenty feet longer than the fuselage and a vertical stabilizer and rudder that appeared to be two sizes too big. Because it was originally designed for carrier operations, the aircraft was usually parked with its wings folded overhead. This smaller profile would allow the aircraft to be parked in tighter spaces. The wings would not have to be unfolded until just before takeoff or a catapult off a carrier deck.

The S-2 syllabus was the first time I deliberately shut down or feathered an engine in flight, not only to practice emergency procedures but to gain confidence the aircraft could fly quite well on one engine all the way to a landing. After ten dual hops with a squadron instructor, I was paired with another student pilot for two solo flights. It was difficult on occasion to sit as copilot and just be helpful, but that's what learning teamwork was all about.

Perfecting basic and radio instrument flying was our next hurdle. This included instrument departures in bad weather, airways flights, and approaches to unfamiliar airfields. We then completed night flying on instruments, tactical and formation flying, and precision flying over water before we began the thirteen flights leading up to carrier qualification on board the *Lexington*.

As in the T-28C, but now in the relative quiet of a closed cockpit, we began simulated carrier landing practices at an airfield set up with the optical landing system. New factors to learn, however, were the added skills needed to execute a practice single-engine landing to a carrier and a single-engine waveoff from a carrier approach that might be required if there was a fouled deck. This phase, again, was exciting, but I have to admit it still did not compare with the anticipation and first thrill of landing the T-28C on board the carrier.

Carrier, commission and wings

The weather over the Gulf of Mexico was unexpectedly poor in late April 1966, so the scheduled launch of S-2s for my carrier qual was delayed one day. As I recall, about twenty cadets and commissioned officers were awaiting the *Lexington* that week. Hitting the boat would mean gold Navy wings for the officers. Cadets completing the carrier qual in the Stoof would be commissioned as ensigns in the Naval Reserve and then receive their wings. Both groups earlier had filled out future assignment "dream sheets" that set their own desires against the greater "needs of the Navy." Within days of completing the carrier qual, all would learn to some extent what fate and the U.S. Navy had in store for them.

On my dream sheet of three flying choices with three location preferences for each, I chose VA or attack as my first choice and Naval Air Station Alameda, California, as the first location. I still had the prop A-1 Skyraider as my dream come true, even though I had been hearing very few new pilots were getting them. As a backup, if the Navy saw fit not to send me to attack, I chose the less aggressive VR or transport role as my second flying choice to pursue as a career. On a whim, I picked VP or patrol as my third choice with Brunswick, Maine; Patuxent River, Maryland; and a place I had never heard of before, Whidbey Island, Washington, as my third location choice.

The weather was still bad on the day we were to launch on the carrier, so aircraft were sent out individually to circle in a holding pattern over the carrier. In my S-2, the instructor and I circled the carrier for two hours without seeing it or the other aircraft circling above and below. With each succeeding aircraft being called in to make approaches from the bottom of the holding pattern, our time finally came.

We broke out of the overcast at about 900 feet and commenced our approach to the carrier. The instructor this time was flying and I was acting as copilot. He demonstrated one touch-and-go and then went around to make an arrested landing. Now it was my turn.

We launched without a catapult and started a lazy left climbing turn to the approach pattern altitude. We lost sight of the carrier several times on the downwind but had it in constant sight on the lefthand turn before calling the "meatball" and beginning our descent on the visual glide path.

My touch-and-go and arrested landings were uneventful and so procedurally correct this time that I avoided owing the LSO a bottle of spirits for causing him any heart burn. Now I could look forward to a commission, a coveted set of gold wings and an assignment where I could continue to fulfill my dreams and fantasies.

Where's Whidbey Island?

I received my gold naval aviator wings on Friday, April 29, 1966, exactly one year and one day after completing simulated bombing runs over Liberty ships in upper Mobile Bay on my first solo flight. Hopefully, this would be a harbinger to an attack assignment in A-1 Skyraiders. I really wouldn't have cared at what location, if I had gotten an attack billet or assignment.

I had been commissioned four days earlier, standing at attention with my right hand raised before the base administration officer. He was a kindly gentleman, making excuses and saying he was sorry it wasn't more of a ceremony, but I really didn't mind—I was on my way.

On Monday, I got an assignment, but it wasn't to an attack squadron. I received orders to Patrol Squadron 17 (VP-17), which was located at Whidbey Island, Washington. As it turned out, being eleventh in placement of twenty-two students getting assignments that week, the needs of the Navy superseded any fantasies I might have had. Instead, I would have to patrol . . . and as it shortly turned out, navigate as well.

Since Whidbey Island was my third location choice of my third flight preference, I went to the base library to find an atlas. I could not find it at first, but there it was, that airplane symbol on a long and narrow island in north Puget Sound just outside a town called Oak Harbor. It was practically in Canada!

The real shock for me, a spanking-new naval aviator raring to fly, was the notification from the base administration office that I had been immediately assigned to VT-29, still at Corpus for two more long months, to learn the skills of an overwater navigator. In patrol aviation, I was to learn, the newest pilot on a crew is the designated navigator. Though he does fly about one-third of each mission, he has the added duty to navigate the aircraft over its assigned course.

Not in my wildest dreams had I ever considered I would have to navigate, and as it turned out, most new aviators who had patrol assignments felt the same way. This consternation was highlighted in a situation I heard about of a disgruntled new aviator who was balking at or otherwise failing the navigation course in hopes of being assigned directly to a squadron as a pilot. I understood later he had to appear before an administrative board that recommended he have his naval aviator certification rescinded. This was a serious situation, but the outcome was not lost on those of us who arrived at "nav" school within a week to seriously begin our new challenge.

Actually, the training was interesting, and made better pilots of us later on in our patrol careers. The most fascinating was celestial navigation—that is, using sextant observations of the sun, moon and stars to plot our positions on the face of the earth. On those days when the celestial bodies failed to show themselves—and that was quite a lot of the time—we learned to plot dead reckoning and to use long-range radio navigation.

In nine flights, about half at night, we navigated over and around the Gulf of Mexico, making the many course and altitude changes that would be the modus operandi of a patrol mission. After completion of the graduation flight, I was ready to navigate myself to San Diego and begin training in the P2V Neptune, my first fleet aircraft.

The ferocious turtle

Texas is big. It took me more than twenty hours to drive across the state on my way to California over the many slow two-lane roads that were the thoroughfares in the mid-1960s. West Texas, with its short rolling hills, was the most challenging. At night, poor dumb jack rabbits would crouch just over the next rise, standing up on their hinds to freeze in place at the glare of oncoming headlights.

I swerved and used my brakes hard through the night, but unfortunately could not avoid one particularly dumb bunny. I had to pull into the town of Alpine at 9 P.M. for some rest, totally exhausted from my first combat mission.

The highways got better beyond El Paso, into New Mexico and Arizona. I stopped at one old service station along the way to check on my rather high engine temperature and was persuaded by a guy who looked like Gabby Hayes to buy a canvas water bag to take along on my engine grill, just in case of a radiator boil over. No doubt, I probably provided a chuckle or two for the locals, seeing a New York-licensed vehicle sufficiently outfitted by L.L. Bean—they would think—to take on the rigors of a hot, desert southwest highway.

San Diego was a pleasant city in 1966, unlike the traffic jam it is today, and the Naval Air Station North Island, adjacent to picturesque Coronado, was my new home for the next five months. I checked into VP-31, the Replacement Air Group (RAG) squadron for those who were to be trained in the P2V Neptune, and began eight weeks of ground school. On my first weekend off after arriving at North Island, I learned a significant part about the history of the venerable aircraft I was about to fly from a most unlikely source.

Any military officer who wanted to have a fun time on a Friday night in the San Diego area was sure to be found at the Marine Corps Recruiting Depot (MCRD) Officers Club bar. It was an incredible social gaggle of younger officers who either wanted to meet with their buddies, or look to socialize with some of the "local natives." It was like a friendly Irish pub, where conversation, camaraderie and story telling were more important than blaring music. An argument or confrontation was rare, it was just a nice place to relax, talk or laugh.

On bar stools next to me on my first visit were two local ladies engaged in a lively conversation. I was with some new found ground school classmates, but being in civilian clothes and looking younger than my years, no doubt, due to the close-cropped haircut, the lady closest to me had to ask what I was doing there. I got over the officer part first—to ensure her I had every right to be there—and went straight to the P2V training I was about to begin. She was pleasantly surprised and warmed up in a motherly sort of way to tell me the story of the most illustrious P2V Neptune in history, the "Truculent Turtle."

I knew well that Neptune was the Roman god of the sea, so I thought, at first, this lady was kidding me about a turtle and we would have a good laugh about it later. But as she started explaining the details in aviation jargon, I got the drift she wasn't telling me a fable, like the tortoise and the hare. Where did this sweet lady get all of this stuff?

It seems the Truculent Turtle, for real, was the first production aircraft built, after the two prototypes. It was modified into a flying gas tank and flown 11,236 miles nonstop from Perth, Australia, to Columbus, Ohio, thereby setting a new world's record for the longest distance without refueling. This took place in September 1946, she told me with pride. When I was two and a half years old, I was thinking to myself.

The Turtle carried over 8,000 gallons of fuel for the planned flight to Washington, D.C., or Bermuda if there was enough gasoline remaining to make it that far, she explained. The takeoff was the first use of Jet Assisted Takeoff (JATO) bottles in a P2V, to ensure the Turtle got off the rather short runway.

The flight plan was going smoothly until the Turtle encountered cold weather and icing over the mountains of the western United States. Having used more fuel in the final portion of the flight than planned, and now fifty-five hours in the air, the crew opted to land at Columbus, short of their goal but a new record, nevertheless. "The record stood for sixteen years, beaten only four years ago by an Air Force B-52 crew," she concluded with real sadness in her voice.

I was flabbergasted by the depth of her knowledge but had wits enough to ask if I could buy her and her girl friend a drink.

It was fourteen years later that my P-3 Orion crew and I were in Pensacola, Florida, and had the chance to visit the Naval Aviation Museum, where we stood on the lawn in back of the main building looking up at the Truculent Turtle, now there on display. No one had to tell me the story, since I had already been well informed.

Back in my room on base that night, I found my well-worn college dictionary. My sweet bar-stool tutor had thought "truculent" meant stalwart. My text, however, showed "fierce, cruel, savage, ferocious, pugnacious and bellicose," as the meaning. I chose ferocious.

In ground school I was beginning to learn that the P2V was more awesome than I had previously thought. The aircraft, though designed primarily for an Antisubmarine Warfare (ASW) role, also was equipped for rocket attack, torpedo attack, mine laying, mast-level depth bombing, horizontal bombing and photo reconnaissance. Maybe this turtle was ferocious, after all.

In ground simulators we trained most of the time for the ASW role. This entailed the crew coordination of many systems on board the aircraft, the deployment of expendable electronic sonobuoys with exacting precision in an ocean environment, and the tactics that solved the submarine's location and course. If necessary, the P2V packed the weapons that could destroy any submarine. Though the first design work for the P2V was initiated in 1941, each succeeding model of the aircraft was upgraded to carry the latest weapons, including nuclear depth charges. Thus, at the request of my future squadron, I attended additional schools at North Island that certified me as a nuclear weapons delivery pilot and a nuclear weapons training officer.

Besides flying low over the water to provide both visual-daylight and nighttime-searchlight shipping surveillance, the Neptune also could triangulate enemy coastal radars and pinpoint their locations while remaining offshore beyond the range of land-based offensive weapons.

I was to fly the last Lockheed-produced model of the Neptune that was originally designated as the P2V-7 but later changed to the SP-2H or "Hotel" model. The aircraft carried a rather large and effective airborne search radar, the APS-20, which in the hands of an experienced operator was phenomenal in its range and clarity. We learned in ground school and it was proven in the air that a low flying P2V could detect a small target at 65 miles, a medium airborne target at 85 miles, and a ship the size of a destroyer at a 200 mile range.

Some of the better radar operators also could pick out the thin, almost invisible, metallic intake and exhaust tubes of a snorkeling submarine at 10 to 15 nautical miles.

All of these capabilities of the P2V that I learned about in ground school would prove to be invaluable to me in short order when I went on patrol in the coastal waters off Vietnam.

My first flight in a Neptune was actually comfortable. The instructor and crew thankfully did not want to overwhelm three of us young aviators at such an early stage with this large "two-turn'in and two-burn'in" aircraft. The SP-2H model definitely was a unique "bird," with two huge Wright compound R-3350 reciprocating engines driving four-bladed, twelve-foot-diameter Hamilton Standard propellers; and two auxiliary Westinghouse J-34 turbojet engines. During the four-hour flight, the instructor only demonstrated normal landings at the runway on San Clemente Island and discussed normal procedures before returning to North Island. My subsequent twenty-three flights over three months were reflective of the two-inch-thick P2V flight manual that contained over five hundred and seventy pages, of which sixty pages were emergency procedures that had to be set to memory. Nearly every flight took hours of study and the use of cue cards to memorize the systems and the critical emergency procedures.

One pleasant flight during the syllabus was an overwater navigation flight from North Island to my future squadron home at Whidbey Island, Washington. With three other "nav" students, two instructor pilots and four other crew members, we took off from North Island and headed northwest out to sea in beautiful California sunshine. While on my navigation segment of the flight off the coast of Oregon, the October weather conditions changed from sun to storm in just a few minutes. Since we had taken off before 6 A.M., most of the crew members were a little foggy-headed, and I was no different. I had requested my third or fourth cup of coffee from the aft station—where the coffee pot was located—and had just heard "Coffee on the wing beam" in my headset when we hit some moderate turbulence. Knowing the cup would not stay for very long on the vibrating wing beam that separated the aircraft fuselage compartments, I unstrapped myself from the navigator's seat and cautiously walked back the short distance to the front of the wing beam, holding on to seats and the side of the narrow flight deck, to reach across the curved beam and rescue the steaming paper cup.

Almost ten hours after takeoff, I was now in the copilot's seat as we marked on top Tatoosh Island off the Olympic Peninsula of Washington state. The four of us had successfully navigated our segments of the flight using combinations of forecast winds over the course, dead reckoning, sextant readings of the sun, radar fixes of the coastline or islands over 100 miles away to the east, location information provided by LORAN (Long Range Navigation) sites on the west coast and radio bearings from airways facilities. The clouds were in layers both high and low, and we only caught glimpses of the land below from time to time during the final airways miles to Whidbey. Yet, we were impressed by the many shades of Northwest green, an "alive look" that contrasted sharply with the mostly-yellow landscape and pollution haze of our departure point. Arriving late in the afternoon, we only had time to go to the exchange for a T-shirt, eat dinner at the base club and get

GENERAL ARRANGEMENT DIAGRAM
(Typical)

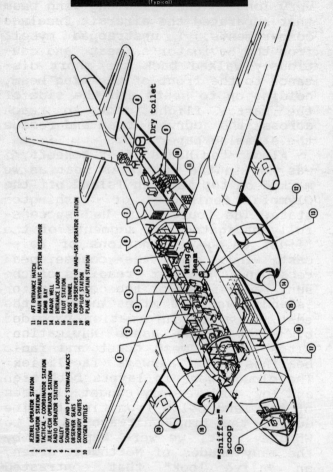

1. JEZEBEL OPERATOR STATION
2. NAVIGATOR STATION
3. TACTICAL - COORDINATOR STATION
4. JULIE-ECM OPERATOR STATION
5. GALLEY
6. SONOBUOY AND PDC STOWAGE RACKS
7. RADIO OPERATOR STATION
8. OBSERVER SEATS
9. SONOBUOY CHUTES
10. OXYGEN BOTTLES
11. AFT ENTRANCE HATCH
12. MAIN HYDRAULIC SYSTEM RESERVOIR
13. BOMB BAY
14. RADAR WELL
15. ENTRANCE LADDER
16. PILOT STATION
17. NOSE TUNNEL
18. MAD OBSERVER OR MAD-ASR OPERATOR STATION
19. COPILOT STATION
20. PLANE CAPTAIN STATION

SP-2H
(U.S. Navy)

some sleep to prepare us for our return trip the next day. Unlike our rainy and windy arrival day, our departure the next morning on the return navigation flight to San Diego was superb. Sunlight and a few billowing clouds greeted us to reveal a beautiful and expansively-timbered landscape with tall snow-capped mountains on the horizon to the east. It hadn't been the primary location I chose on my dream sheet, but being chosen for Whidbey Island was one of the better decisions the Navy made for me, and in spite of me.

To the breakwater for dinner

About halfway through the P2V syllabus, my class and I were assigned to the Survival, Escape, Resistance and Evasion (SERE) school at North Island, and its desert training and simulated Prisoner-Of-War (POW) camp at Warner Springs, California. The POW training definitely left an impression on me . . . I had a black eye to nurse for three weeks, afterwards.

As a kid who grew up in New York City—some called it an asphalt jungle—I was fascinated by my first day of ground school at North Island. We had been through a few days of survival training in Florida to get the semitropical aspect of survival, but this adventure was to introduce us to the seashore and desert environments.

After a half-day of ground school

with no lunch—just liquids to keep us going—we were bused to the rocky breakwater area at the entrance of San Diego Bay to begin our seashore training. We foraged the breakwater and seashore for several hours accompanied by instructors who showed us what edible things we could have for the picking. We also were shown the basic way to capture crabs from the waters off the rocks, but we weren't too successful, at first, until someone fashioned a triangular scoop from debris we found on the shoreline. We were beginning to get the picture about our survival situation.

By sundown, our class of about fifty trainees had a small assortment of snails, limpets, mussels and some of the ugliest crabs I had ever seen. We boiled the mess in an iron pot and picked at it without a lot of gusto. Though we were hungry, I think our selective sampling of raw edible species, especially the limpets, left most of us with little or no appetite for more. Feeling the first effects of weakness, we slept soundly on the beach that night, each wrapped in a parachute canopy.

Recovered somewhat the next morning—most likely from our own body fat—we were bused to the Navy's training facility near Warner Springs, a semiarid area north of San Diego to learn foraging, shelter construction and overland navigation. We were given some preliminary classroom work and cautioned about the rattlesnakes in the area, and then we began foraging for small animals and edible plants. Since many classes used the same area each year, there literally were no edible plants or animals to be found, but we were obliged to look anyway. One party of foragers found a small rattlesnake which they decided to leave alone—to let it become a big rattlesnake one day and be someone else's meal, or so their story went.

Back in our designated camp before sunset, our instructors gave each group of ten trainees one live rabbit and pigeon to eat that night. In a group of ten people, you would have thought one would have been a farm boy who was used to preparing livestock to eat. Not in my group. No one wanted anything to do with killing or preparing the animals. By virtue of being the second senior officer in my group, even as lowly as an ensign, this New York City boy was ordered by a lieutenant to lead by example and prepare one of the animals. I choose to prepare the pigeon and ordered one of my more macho subordinates to prepare the rabbit.

I had never done this before, but I recalled from my youth the woman next door ringing the neck of a duck, a necessity resulting from a unwanted Easter present that had grown too big and messy for her back yard. With this accomplished, I began dry plucking my bird. This was a tedious job, and the lieutenant had the gall after I was finished to tell me I should have dropped the bird in boiling water for a spell to make the job go easier. As far as my superior was concerned, I thought the first rule of leadership was not to ask your subordinates to do something you weren't willing to do yourself.

With my rather large and dull survival knife, I made a real mess of gutting the bird and cutting off its head. Yet, I had visions of a nice roasted breast of pigeon for my group to savor. My weak-culinary daydream was dashed when an instructor walking through our camp insisted I boil the bird in a coffee can provided—and throw in the head for good measure.

I know there are people who would kill for boiled pigeon, but I have to be honest; seeing the eyes roll up to the top of the coffee can and breathing in that mess I had on me in the desert sun made me sick. It was all that I could do—being the cook and all—to keep from letting the dry heaves incapacitate me. For months afterward, I could not touch anything that looked like or smelled like pigeon, including turkey and chicken.

Though we were into our second day without a regular meal, just as we had at the shore, my group ate only sparingly from our pots of boiled pigeon and rabbit. We were only too glad a little before sunset to construct a parachute tent and roll up in additional parachutes for a long night's rest.

We awoke chilled on our third morning, a little from the temperature and a little from a lack of nourishment. The task for the day was a three-mile overland navigation hike and return to camp, and as before, we were kept in our smaller groups of ten to make the going less crowded. With no food scheduled for the day, we also would forage as we went, in hopes of having something to eat when we returned to camp. Though it was October in Southern California, the heat of the sun was our biggest burden. Being out in the noon day sun—as mad dogs and Englishmen know—brought several in my group close to fainting, but as in flying by committee, our team maintained a pace and took breaks as often as needed to get everyone through the course. Back in the tent area late that afternoon we were all surprised and delighted by a low-flying S-2 "Stoof" which buzzed our site and dropped five tins of corned beef by parachute.

The senior officer in our larger class, a commander, dispersed one can to each group of ten with the proviso that it be shared equally. Being the junior officer, my lieutenant ordered me, again, to cut the meat in equal shares. He was getting too used to this delegation of authority stuff.

I opened the can under the stares of ten hungry men. Not surprisingly, none of us was adverse to corned beef. Yet, after all the time and effort it took to figure out equal shares of meat, I could not come up with anything larger than approximately one cubic-inch per person. The gelatin, which in any other situation would have been discarded, was a big hit with the few that got it.

A little before sunset, the entire camp was called together and briefed about the evasion course we would be going through that night. After successful completion of that, the next morning we were scheduled for a daytime evasion course leading to immediate incarceration in the prisoner-of-war camp . . . unless we escaped to a place called "Freedom Village" for a short reprieve.

Escape, evasion and POW camp

Our evasion course on the third night of our SERE school was a straight forward problem. How to infiltrate a whole gaggle of people through a narrow corridor of brush past lighted guard towers. It became apparent to all of us huddled at the beginning of the course, that we would have to stagger the large number of people in our group or become bottlenecked in the obvious, better routes that had cover. Since we were not being actively pursued or opposed, it was one of the more "fun" things we did in the cooler night air.

The next morning was a different

story. No longer in groups, we were released in staggered individual starts to a wider and longer evasion course with a goal of arriving at Freedom Village, a concrete foundation about one mile away through sparse brush. We were going to be actively pursued in our attempt by enemy soldiers, and if captured early in the course, we would be taken immediately to the simulated prisoner-of-war camp. Those evading capture would get a cup of water upon arrival at Freedom Village.

Growing up in The Big Apple, I was not exactly a frontiersman, but I could see that there were just too many people in groups close to the starting line. Not many were moving out to disperse. I chose to take a chance and sprint far to the left boundary of the course before beginning a stop, look, listen and creep tactic. After several hundred yards, I found myself alone, but I could hear trucks in the distance to my right and the apparent shouts of guards barking orders and insults to those captured early on. My strategy had been working well for about a half a mile, when I caught a glimpse of an armed man in green fatigues coming my way.

I was already off the path and scrambling, at least, twenty feet underneath a low thicket of brush when he began to bellow, "Come out, I see you." My heart was pounding so hard I could hear it in my ears, but I wasn't about to make it easy for him. He'd have to crawl under and into my thicket to get me. After a few more verbal threats, it became apparent that he didn't know exactly where I was and he had no intention of crawling anywhere to look for me . . . or a potential rattlesnake.

It was more than ten minutes before I moved again, slowly crawling back to the edge of the thicket and looking cautiously for the guard. I was hot, dusty, confused, physically weak, and had to reorient myself with the terrain I had been crossing before I dove under the brush. When I got my bearings, I started moving again, keeping the sun on my left shoulder.

I must have gone about another half-mile when the landscape changed from clumps of thick brush to a more open area with few places to hide. After looking and listening for several minutes, I ran for the cover of a downed log at the base of a tree twenty yards in the distance. Jumping over the log, I startled and was face to face with a coyote who had not been paying attention to my approach but licking something on the ground. It took about a second for both of us to depart our mutual cover, comically in the same direction for about ten feet before we got to the open ground.

Shortly thereafter, I saw an unarmed but uniformed man standing in the distance above what appeared to be a pit. Upon closer observation, the pit was a concrete foundation with twenty or so happy evaders sitting inside savoring their prize cup of water. I must have taken a long time to finish the course, for I had only 30 seconds to sit down and chug my half cup of warm water before Freedom Village was surrounded by nasty comrades who ordered and pushed us into arriving trucks.

Amid shouts, insults and threats, we were herded out of our truck after a ten-minute ride to the receiving area of the simulated POW camp. Before entering the camp's inner compound, we were ordered to take off our outer clothes and have them searched. Then into the hot and dusty enclosure we were thrust to put our clothes back on and stand at attention while the other prisoners' belongings were searched. Unlike the movies or visions we might have had of a POW camp, ours was a small square enclosure. There were no above-ground buildings in the compound, just two bunkers buried in the sandy soil. The perimeter was a high barbed wire fence that was guarded by machine gun-armed sentries located atop wooden towers in opposite corners of the compound.

There were many guards in the compound, at first, though only a few were shouting intimidating orders. The quiet ones were closely observing us, trying to pick out those who could be easily persuaded.

As a group, our most senior officers had been removed early on, no doubt, for intensive abuse, while the junior officers and enlisted were kept together for observation.

In retrospect, I believe a flub of mine during this observation period would spur the guards in short order to give me a lot of "special" treatment that included a little bit of carrot and a lot of stick.

A small, big mistake

Standing at attention in the hot sunshine of the POW compound, I looked around as much as I could without drawing undue attention. Unfortunately, it appeared the vast majority of other prisoners with me were people who had not been in my smaller group, so I didn't know any of them. After standing at attention for a rather long period of time, we were ordered by a comrade to fall out. Luckily, because we had not planned it this way, we had the presence of mind as a group not to respond. Threats did not alter the situation until the guard reluctantly placed one of our own junior officers in charge.

With a command from our own leadership, we broke ranks and walked the compound to presumably clean it up. When ordered back into ranks by a comrade, our own officer took a sufficient amount of time to call, "Fall in." It was during this time I had the stupidity to suggest to the man standing next to me to step back somewhat to form a straight line. A quiet, observing comrade immediately noticed this potential for cooperation and physically forced me out of ranks away from the group and over to a corner of the compound.

He told me to "Relax." I knew I was in for it. My quiet suggestion to the man in ranks was all he needed to see that this young officer had the potential to serve his purposes. This friendly comrade sat me down and told me I would not have to go through any of this unpleasant experience if I was willing to just not take sides. If I did not oppose the guards, I would be left alone. He offered me a cigarette as a sign of his good faith, but I made no motion to accept it. I neither looked at him nor answered him. No matter what was going to come my way, I decided I had better begin resisting right then.

When I refused to accept any favor or promise of light treatment, the carrot was withdrawn and the guard grabbed me by the neck and arm, forcibly running me back to the men standing at attention in ranks, and trying to use me like a battering ram to knock over some of my fellow prisoners. My one-time mentor angrily shook a finger at me suggesting I would regret my refusal of his most-considerate offer.

I don't know how long we stood in the hot sun at attention, but it was long enough for several of those in our ranks to pass out and fall to the ground. When that occurred, they would be carried by other prisoners to an underground bunker, where presumably a real corpsman would examine them and let them shake off the heat in the cooler temperature.

The heat and our lack of water was taking its toll, yet groups of five prisoners at a time were being removed from the compound for who knew what additional treatment. How far could our tormentors go in carrying out a simulated POW environment? I was about to find out.

"You, you, you, you and you." The last finger was pointed at me, but somehow I didn't think I was going to be the least. We were tired and thirsty, but they still double-time marched us to a row of small boxes baking in the hot sun. Each of us was forced to squat cross-legged in one of the boxes. The lids were then slammed shut on top of us. Obviously, since the lid did not slam hard enough on my slender frame, my particular guard immediately reopened my box, forced me out of it, and placed another smaller wooden box inside to fill it in. Now the lid slammed on my back.

It helped to be physically fit and flexible that day. The guards outside admonished all those inside to speak up when they rapped on the top of the box with their rifle butts.

For whatever reason, I decided I was not going to answer the guards, and if need be, faint in the box before I would appear to cooperate again. On two occasions over approximately twenty minutes in the box, a guard rapped his rifle butt on my lid. Both times when I would not answer, he would open the box, pull my head up by what little hair that I had, slap me hard for not cooperating and slam the lid shut again. There was more to come.

It was hard to breathe in the heat, and fainting was a real possibility, but I got through that episode before being pulled out of the box by two men, who pushed and forced me into a nearby room. I was tired, thirsty, weak, and I really don't remember the questions they asked me. All I recall is telling them my name, rank and serial number. Well, that certainly wasn't good enough for them. I responded in my most polite New Yorkese, but they still "beat the crap" out of me; mostly cuffs to the face and upper torso. As a kid from the city who beat up other kids as much as I was beaten up, this really wasn't a big deal. I really thought their tactics were going to be more psychologically-persuasive than physical.

They took turns with me, bounced me off the springy-plywood walls a couple of times, but one of them had more of a fist than the other and caught my right eye with a hard punch. My jaw also felt a little dislocated. So much for simulations!

That wasn't so bad, I thought, as they dragged me out of the room toward the compound. But, they took a little detour back to the boxes. I guess they would try this exercise on me one more time. I was in just a short time when the box was opened by someone who pulled my hair again, but this time to examine my swollen face. "He'll live," was the comrade medic's snide remark, as the lid was slammed down again. However, they must have felt sorry for me this time because they didn't take the time to put in a filler box.

Back in the compound after my special "welcome aboard reception," I had a relatively free time. We were neither allowed to go into the bunkers to get out of the sun, nor congregate in large groups. We had not been given water since that morning, so there were many zombie-like prisoners roaming around the small dusty compound. As I was walking the perimeter looking at the layout and fantasizing about escaping, all of the prisoners in the compound were startled by an air raid siren and shouts from the guards in the towers and in the yard to get on the ground. We did this as the tower guards began firing blanks in their machine guns to the east as two A-1 Skyraiders in formation made one and then another high-speed low pass over the high fences.

On the second pass, one of the "Spads" dropped small paper leaflets into the compound warning our captors to treat their soon-to-arrive squadron executive officer, commander so-and-so, kindly or suffer the consequences. I'm sure the commander was shown one of those leaflets in short order, but there must have been hell to pay for the privilege to see it.

In our sorry state, it was an incredible thrill to see, hear and feel the power of those beautiful Skyraiders as they made their passes. I may be just imagining it but my fatigue seemed to go out of me after this unexpected but thundering visit.

I got a jolt a little later that afternoon, as a guard led my camping group's lieutenant around on all fours, like a big dog on the end of a rope leash. I was mortified and sorry to see this, for as short as this simulation was in hours, it was painful to see one of my camping group giving in to the power of intimidation.

Toward sunset, our senior officers were marched back into the compound, looking haggard and abused. Later we heard their treatment had been much more intensive owing to their rank and future responsibilities. This was the first time since our arrival at Warner Springs two days previously that we were all together as a group.

Our senior officer, the soon-to-be executive officer of the A-1 squadron, was now in charge and he began organizing our operation as it suited him and not the comrades. Somehow the ensign, again, was assigned to the cooking duty. My fame as a boiled-pigeon chef must have preceded me into this POW scenario. Even at this late hour, we still had not been given anything to drink. As I set about to cut the issued beef into cubes and mix it with the cut potatoes, my mouth and tongue were the driest they had ever been, but I dared not steal any of the water that the comrades brought in for the cooking pot.

It was only after our food was ready and each individual got a little liquid drippings with his portion, that the guards gave out a limited water ration. After eating, all of the prisoners were ordered into the bunkers to rest.

We were rudely but happily roused at about 3 A.M. and told the exercise was over. After forming up, we marched out of the compound a short distance to a debriefing building. After being seated, I looked around the group to see if the lieutenant, my former camping group superior, had made it. He had not.

After the debrief, we were loaded into buses and driven back to North Island. The trip took about three hours, including a ferry ride to Coronado. Few awoke from their deep sleeps until the bus arrived in front of the SERE School office. The former POWs had to be forcibly roused to receive their diplomas and transfers back to their squadrons, stations, or ships.

For the next three Friday nights at the MCRD Officers Club bar, when prodded, I would relive the story of how I had received a black eye from a comrade interrogator.

I was back in my RAG squadron in early November 1966 and scheduled for eleven more training flights in the SP-2H. These were more pilot-crew coordination flights than pilot syllabus hops. It wasn't going to be long before my assignment to my fleet squadron, which had already begun its six-month deployment to southern Japan, with a detachment of aircraft to Tan Son Nhut in Vietnam. In my subsequent flights prior to departure overseas, I would have to learn the finesse it would take to successfully fly by committee.

The military in time of war takes no holidays, and so on Christmas Day 1966, a replacement tactical coordinator and I departed Travis Air Force Base, California, on a DC-8 charter flight to the Philippines. Somewhere over the northern Pacific, as the aircraft flew west of the International Date Line, we lost Christmas Day earlier than we would have normally. After a stop in the Tokyo area for fuel, we arrived at Clark Air Force Base in the early evening of the 26th. Our fleet unit, Patrol Squadron 17, though originally deployed to Japan, had been moved again after only three months to the Philippines. We stayed overnight at Clark and called our squadron duty office the next morning. The duty officer informed us that a C-47 was already enroute from our base at Sangley Point to Clark and probably could give us a flight back. We met the crew as they were dropping off passengers and cargo at the Clark terminal, and they indicated it wouldn't be any problem for them to take us on the 100-mile flight back to historic Sangley Point.

Though still groggy-eyed after checking in, both the new tactical coordinator and I accepted an invitation from the off-going duty officer to join him on a visit to Manila, about 10 miles away. This would be an easy trip on a liberty barge which sailed hourly during the day from the Sangley Point pier to the American embassy dock on the Manila waterfront. The old city was exciting, loud and very colorful, especially the "Jeepneys," the gaudy and festooned local communal taxies.

After returning to our base, our new found friend told us about the routine and alerted us to especially review the flight schedule every day—no day was a holiday unless you were on leave.

I had been in the squadron less than twelve hours and my name was already on the flight schedule as third pilot-navigator for a flight early the next morning to Iwakuni, Japan, where the squadron had been recently deployed. The eight-hour flight to Japan would be mostly airways with just a little navigation over water between islands. As a history buff, I was keenly aware that in just those short hours, there would be many momentous sights to see from the air: Corregidor, the Battan Peninsula, Lingayen Gulf,

Okinawa, Nagasaki and Hiroshima.

Our destination, Iwakuni, also played a large role during World War II. Though it was in late 1966 a U.S. Marine Corps Air Station, it had previously been an Imperial Japanese base that trained Zero and kamikaze pilots. The first leg of this flight was such a historical adventure—and an important learning experience for the new kid on the crew.

Relief tube was no relief

Since the P2V is not a pressurized aircraft, our initial cruise altitude of only 6,000 feet to Japan allowed a fantastic view of the World War II sites we would be flying over. Though I was the designated navigator and third pilot for the flight, I found quite a lot of time to leave my navigation station and crawl to the plexiglas bow observer's seat to look straight down on the history beneath our wings. A little over four hours into the flight, we marked on top Okinawa and were heading north on airways into a "Siberian Express" of below-freezing weather that had been predicted by forecasters.

Halfway between Okinawa and southern Kyushu, I was called by the co-pilot to come to the cockpit and relieve him for an hour. Since I had been on the navigation table for a few hours before this and had received many "Coffee on the wing beam" calls in my headset, I thought it wise to use the flight deck relief tube before I went to the cockpit.

Now, all of my P2V flight experience, to date, had been in southern California, a quick trip to Whidbey Island in October, and this, my first operational flight which originated in the tropical Philippines. I didn't know it at the time, but I was in for my first unique Neptune experience, one, I guess, everyone on board had to learn for himself. I got on the microphone and "rogered" the request for me to come up to the cockpit, adding I'd be a minute at the relief tube. I had used the relief tube system many times before but never in the below-freezing temperatures of southern Japan in the winter.

The procedure was simple enough for the flight deck behind the cockpit, one of three locations in the aircraft where you could find a relief tube. All a crew member had to do was raise the hinged wooden lid that protected the top of the hydraulic service center reservoir, feel around in the dark for the five inch cone-shaped black plastic receptacle attached to a rubber tube, lean against the lid to keep it upright, pull up the bottom zipper of your flight suit (we called them zoom bags), point your appendage into the cone, and with your other hand hold a spring-loaded heater switch in the "on" position for one minute. In turbulent weather, the only option with your hands already occupied was to spread your legs farther apart to get a little more stability and make sure your aim was good. Yet, even in calm weather, owing to the dark color of the cone, the dark location of the tube, the awkward leaning and switch-holding process, one would tend to tinkle on one's hand, no matter what. Was the spring-loaded heater switch a safety concern or a sadistic plan?

The frigid temperature brought on a whole new challenge. My cone and tube were still full nearly to the top of the rim after following all the exacting procedures. I couldn't see it, but I could feel it.

To make matters worse, another crew member shouted back to me that they were waiting on me up in the cockpit. I shouted back my predicament; there wasn't much I could do about it. Did he want to help?

Not wanting to get involved in these personal matters, the crewman just offered advice: To continue holding the cone high, keep depressing the heater switch to "on" in hope it would eventually melt the yellow ice in the aft venturi and drain out. It took two more long minutes in this unwieldy position, with careful checking from time to time for the liquid to drain down and out of the aircraft.

Up in the cockpit, my story to the old timers elicited just a couple of chuckles.

" No matter how bad you have to go, don't fill it up all at once, just a little at a time. Make sure its going down before you finish," the sages advised. At twenty-two years of age, I was still being potty-trained.

I had been overseas only two days, and in that short time I had completed my first fleet-operational flight, logged over eight hours of flight time, covered 1,400 nautical miles and visited the Philippines and southern Japan. The next morning was clear and cold, and our return flight, which I navigated from Okinawa to northern Luzon, was uneventful, including several episodes at the cold, unforgiving and finicky relief tube.

I was to remain on the ground for only two days to meet with the Commanding Officer (CO), start my ground jobs as public affairs and assistant personnel officer and to meet with as many other officers and personnel as were still at Sangley Point. On New Year's eve, I was scheduled as a passenger with a squadron aircrew repositioning to Saigon with their aircraft to begin "Market Time" patrol operations. The squadron had assigned me as an on-call navigator/third pilot ready to fly with any crew that needed me. Thus, three and a half hours after takeoff from the Philippines, I watched with anticipation the sandy coastline of Vung Tau, Vietnam, come into view beneath my feet as I sat in the plexiglas bow station of the aircraft flying northwest to Saigon.

Chapter 3

VIETNAM

I had seen it graphically on TV over several years. Now I was there—Vietnam on the last day of 1966.

It took less than thirty minutes from flying over the coast before we were on an instrument approach to Tan Son Nhut Airport, just four miles from downtown Saigon.

A squadron detachment had been deployed there since October to participate in "Operation Market Time," and for other tasked combat-support missions. I was in just a little bit of awe as we taxied into our flight line area on steel Marston matting and saw five other squadron P2Vs looking smart and lined up facing out . . . probably for a quick getaway.

A maintenance chief was standing off in the distance with his arms folded, no doubt, looking over the aircraft, anticipating the number of "gripes" or maintenance problems the patrol plane commander would write up to be worked off before the next flight.

After the huge props came to a complete stop, the crew began to unload their personal gear and some spare parts the maintenance personnel had ordered from Sangley. The crew's officers threw their bags next to a weird-looking elongated crew-cab pickup truck that had a fenced cage on the back. A maintenance petty officer told me this was the officers' transportation into Saigon where the billet or housing unit was located. The enlisted lived in the Navy's Battlecreek Apartment in Cholon, so they would take a different ride. The same petty officer laughed as he described how the junior officers had to ride in the back cage, locked in from the outside; a definite head-scratcher for me when I imagined an ambush. But, who was I to say anything, the new kid on the block, fresh "in-country" and an ensign, at that.

The pilots from the crew that I had flow in with began to walk away from the pickup truck and motioned me to follow them.

"Come on, we're going down the ramp to see the bird that got hit." This I had to see. We all walked on the uneven steel matting to the last P2V in the line—one that had a jagged two-foot-diameter hole in the side of the fuselage, forward of the leading edge of the wing. Just three weeks earlier in the pre-dawn hours, Viet Cong guerrillas had launched a surprise attack along the squadron line. As mortar shells began to fall among the P2Vs parked in the long line, an enemy squad ran in front of the aircraft, throwing grenades underneath the wings and firing automatic weapons. When the first shells began to fall in the line area, the unarmed maintenance workers dove into several small sandbag bunkers.

Incredibly, no squadron personnel were injured and most of the grenades were duds, but one mortar shell found its mark on the aircraft we were inspecting. The explosion blew a large hole in the side and caused heavy damage to the wiring, mostly in the main electrical load center.

Later on, I learned the circuits were carefully reconnected and tested, the hole repaired with temporary stringers, sheet aluminum, pop rivets and duct tape, and the aircraft was flown back to the Philippines where major repairs were conducted. The aircraft was back in operation within weeks.

The fast trip into Saigon in the "paddy wagon" was guaranteed to be an adventure. Being forewarned was no comfort when I was motioned to sit in the back cage. I wasn't alone, however, but that wasn't any comfort, either. I could see out and the Vietnamese along the road could see in, but I could not have gotten out in an emergency because the cage had been locked from the outside.

"Anyway, we've never been ambushed," offered one of the officers, smugly, as he got into the passenger side of the truck's front seat.

The truck dropped all of us off at a small apartment building that contained about twelve rooms in three stories. The entrance was piled high with sandbags, both as protection for a diesel generator located just outside the front door and for a small sentry post that was manned at night by an armed enlisted member from the squadron. The Viet Cong were becoming adept at driveby grenade and satchel charge attacks from fast-moving motorscooters within the city.

Since I was not a member of a regular crew, I had to hot bunk it for a couple of days in a small room in the front of the apartment facing the street. You could call it the blast-zone room . . . with a view. Probably just another perk of being a junior officer. While Lieutenant X was out on his thirteen- to fifteen-hour patrol evolution, I slept in his bed, just throwing down a sheet on top of his and sleeping under a blanket. Though this was a hot, tropical clime, this crew had managed to commandeer a small air conditioner that kept the room slightly cool, but sticky and smelling of mildew.

Getting used to being with crews that were always on the run, even when they were supposed to be resting, I changed immediately into civilian clothes and went along with the officers I had flown into Saigon with to walk the streets of the city. With the new year just hours away, we strolled the city's wide boulevards to The Rex, a roof top club in the heart of the downtown area designated exclusively for American and allied officers. The separate bar and restaurant were quite pleasant and a little incongruous for me; all these delights, good food and drink, right in the middle of a war zone. The canopied roof provided shade, while the open sides allowed any breezes to pass through and provide some cooling. The view from the top was spectacular. I could see the Continental Hotel, the premier place to be since the French colonial days; the impressive Roman Catholic cathedral, the infamous Tu Do Street where Americans were, no doubt, buying beautiful young ladies a "Saigon tea," and a huge brown statue of two soldiers, one behind the other, charging the white city hall building before it. In late 1966, the word among those at The Rex was the statue depicted an American advisor leading the charge, with his South Vietnamese counterpart behind and on his heels.

With no one even considering to waste their time watching the TV series "Combat" on the television behind the bar, my fellow squadron mates talked, ate and drank the day away. We stayed for the floor show, a fantastic Philippine band that could perfectly mimic every popular American song of the day, but had difficulty speaking English to announce the numbers. Their music was the crescendo that lead up to the "10, 9, 8, 7 . . ." before all hell broke loose on the periphery of the city for miles around. The thunder of artillery and staccato discharges of small arms announced to everyone that a new year of war had begun. There were no other fireworks, per se.

I got back to the apartment with the other crew members by 1 A.M. to cautiously review the posted flight schedule. Neither I nor the crew would be flying until very early on January 2, so we could all rest through another day.

Operation Market Time

Patrol Squadron 17 had been posted to Saigon in October 1966 for a six-month detachment to participate in "Operation Market Time." To fulfill this task, the squadron regularly supplied seven aircraft and rotated crews from its earlier deployment base in Japan and later from the Philippines.

Market Time was a tremendous and successful effort instituted in early 1965 by the U.S. Joint Chiefs of Staff with the concurrence of the South Vietnamese government to stop, search, and seize vessels not clearly engaged in innocent passage inside the three-mile limit of the Republic of Vietnam's territorial waters." Moreover, patrol aviation would quickly become an integral part of this seemingly exclusive waterborne effort.

When America became involved in South Vietnam in the early 1960s, most of the insurgency was inflicted by indigenous communist Viet Cong. Though a trickle of arms and ammunition had been supplied through various means by North Vietnam and other communist counties, the guerrillas, for the most part, had to rely upon captured weapons and leftovers from the earlier Viet Minh. To exert even greater pressure on the south to capitulate, the communist North Vietnamese government in 1964 made an important decision to arm the Viet Cong with more powerful and standardized weapons, especially the AK-47 Soviet-designed assault rifle. In order for the new weapons to have any effect, the north also had to commit to a reliable delivery strategy. With 1,200 miles of coastline for the South Vietnamese to defend, the north decided it would have the most success infiltrating arms by sea.

The commitment of the north to smuggle huge amounts of arms and ammunition by ship into the south was apparent as early as February 1965 when a U.S. Army helicopter flying the central coast area came upon a large camouflaged vessel in Vung Ro Bay. When the contact was passed on to the Navy's coastal zone headquarters, the ship was engaged, sunk, and later found to contain a large supply of arms and equipment for the Viet Cong. Nearby on the mainland, the Navy also found a huge cache of buried supplies. Obviously, large enemy ships were infiltrating coastal South Vietnam undetected to supply insurgent forces.

American advisors were quick to deduce the North Vietnamese plan and rapidly set up an operation that would deny the enemy getting large amounts of weapons by sea. In March 1965, a conference concluded that coastal junk traffic was accounting for a small amount of arms infiltration. The greatest amount was coming on trawlers, usually steel-hulled, that sailed in plain sight in international waters without national flags. The trawlers would make high-speed, perpendicular approaches at night to the coast of South Vietnam to unload, run aground on the beach or camouflage themselves against the jungle or shoreline vegetation for future unloading.

To end the trawler infiltrations, Operation Market Time was set into motion as a coordinated sea blockade of U.S. Navy, Coast Guard, South Vietnamese and allied ships, and U.S. patrol aircraft. The closer the larger trawlers got to the coast of South Vietnam, the easier it was for them to successfully make a high-speed run in the dark to a predetermined rendezvous point with the insurgents. If aircraft could detect the trawlers while they were far out to sea and coordinate a reception party for them as they approached the coast, the arms and ammunition that the north wanted to supply by sea would be nipped in the bud. The U.S. Army's General William Westmorland estimated that before 1965, when Market Time began, seventy per cent of the enemy's supplies arrived by sea. Though only time would tell, the ultimate success of Market Time was North Vietnam's later dramatic change in strategy from seaborne infiltration of arms and ammunition to reliance upon the many roads that made up the greater Ho Chi Minh Trail system.

VP-17's operations in Vietnam began as far back as August 1964 when it was called upon to provide air ASW coverage to fleet task force ships cruising from the Okinawa area to the South China Sea following the Tonkin Gulf Crisis. Shortly thereafter, as was customary, the squadron rotated back to Whidbey Island having completed a six-month deployment in the region. It was replaced by another patrol squadron which would remain until VP-17 was back again in six months to continue its flight operations in WestPac (Western Pacific.)

Operation Market Time had only been in operation two months when VP-17 deployed in 1965 to Iwakuni, Japan, and sent a detachment of aircraft and crews to Saigon. Though it did not discover any trawlers that year, it logged thousands of hours of flight time in three hundred missions along the coast of South Vietnam, from the Cambodian sea frontier to the 17th parallel separating the north and the south.

Up to December 1966, when I joined VP-17, squadron aircraft flying Market Time operations had accounted for numerous suspicious vessels being shadowed and reported, but no arms and ammunition captured. A typical mission involved the effective teamwork of a nine-member crew taking off from Tan Son Nhut at a gross weight of 81,500 pounds to fly over the jungle area to the coast and begin an eight to eleven hour flight, depending on the number of radar or visual contacts encountered and observed. Because this was a twenty-four hours per day operation, every time one aircraft was returning to base, another was reporting "on station." Since South Vietnam had such a long coastline, missions were usually broken into two surveillance regions, with one aircraft per region. Day and night, calm weather or typhoon, there were aircraft on station making indentification passes on trawler-size or larger vessels from an altitude of usually only 200 feet above the waves.

A suspicious ship to an experienced flight crew was one that displayed no nationality or an odd nationality for the region, was not rigged properly for its type of construction, or its course placed it in a position to make a high-speed run for the South Vietnam coast under the cover of darkness. Though the North Vietnamese were continuing to infiltrate smaller amounts of arms on junks in the coastal areas, they relied upon the

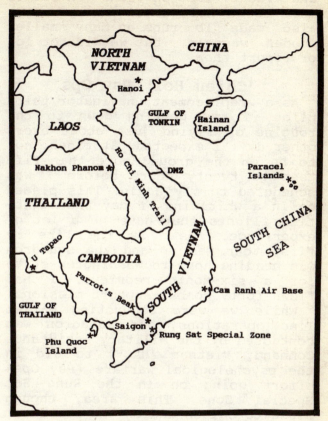

Market Time patrol area

steel-hulled vessels with tons of weapons on board to bluff their way into the coastline.

In this my first "tour" on patrol, a typical nine-hour flight involved a ladder-search pattern of either the north or south half of the South

Vietnam coastline, making low passes and identification runs on 100 or more large hull radar contacts. We also made ID runs on many smaller wooden vessels, but we did not log or report them.

'Chieu Hoi' Psy Ops

As a replacement navigator/third pilot, I was getting down to the routine of flying just about every other day. I expected, at times, not to be on the ground more than fifteen to twenty hours before I was scheduled to fly again. This placed me in a whirlwind of day and nighttime flights that gave me a lot of experience, fast. By the time my first tour was up and the squadron was heading home to Washington state for a six-month reprieve, I had flown forty combat-support missions.

While we were conducting Market Time operations, our squadron was contacted by the Military Assistance Command, Vietnam (MACV) to aid in the psychological warfare (Psy Ops) effort going on in the Rung Sat Special Zone. This area, though close to Saigon and on the route our aircraft took to the coast, was an intensive staging area for the Viet Cong and their North Vietnamese Army (NVA) advisors. Ground attacks on the periphery had not diminished the strength of the enemy within the zone as the jungle canopy, hundreds of miles of canals, swamps and muck made it impossible to successfully raid with a large force. The Vietnamese who lived in the area called it the "Forest of Assassins" due to its past history as a haven for smugglers, bandits and renegades.

Since ground attacks and overwhelming airpower had failed to dislodge the enemy from the Rung Sat Zone, the American leadership in Saigon planned a intensive strategy for the region that actually involved less manpower. To strip away the jungle canopy that hid the enemy, the Air Force began an air-sprayed defoliation program on those sections of the seven-hundred square mile mangrove swamp that were most useful to the guerrillas. After this was initiated, U.S. Navy Seal units were infiltrated into the swamp to

Front of the Chieu Hoi leaflet

ambush and interdict the enemy with hit-and-run tactics. Any large caches of arms or ammunition that were found were either detonated on site or marked for an air strike.

Our role in this operation was minor, but we were enthusiastic to supply one cog in a Psy Ops wheel that might have played a role in

> # ĐỒNG-BÀO GIA-ĐỊNH
>
> Lực-lượng Chánh-phủ và Đồng-minh đang đánh bại Cộng-sản tại khắp chiến-trường, gây cho chúng nhiều tổn-thất nặng-nề về nhân-mạng, võ-khí và quân-dụng.
>
> Không thể công-khai đương đầu với những lực-lượng hùng-hậu của Chánh-phủ và Đồng-minh, Việt-cộng đang tìm cách tránh né vào các nhà cửa, vườn tược, ruộng nương của đồng-bào tại các Xã, Ấp trong tỉnh Gia-định làm địa-bàn pháo-kích vào các cơ-sở và các căn-cứ của Chánh-phủ và Đồng-minh.
>
> Đồng-bào cần phải ý-thức rằng các hành-động kể trên của Việt-cộng sẽ đem đến nhiều tai họa cho đồng-bào vì nếu bị pháo-kích, lực-lượng của Chánh-phủ và Đồng-minh sẽ khám-phá dễ-dàng vị-trí đặt súng của Việt-cộng để tiêu-diệt chúng và do đó, đồng-bào cũng sẽ bị vạ lây.
>
> Để tránh tai họa đem đến cho mình, đồng-bào hãy bí-mật tố-cáo ngay với cơ-quan Chánh-quyền hoặc đồn bốt gần nhứt những nơi có Việt-cộng trú-ẩn, chôn dấu võ-khí, quân-dụng.
>
> ĐỪNG CHẦN-CHỜ NỮA, đây là một dịp tốt để đồng-bào giúp Chánh-phủ tiêu-diệt bọn Việt-cộng hầu bảo-đảm

Back of Chieu Hoi leaflet

Viet Cong or NVA defections. With defoliation and ambush operations going on, VP-17 was given the task of dropping paper Chieu Hoi leaflets at altitudes of usually 2,000 feet over the Rung Sat jungle from aircraft that were outbound from Saigon to the South China Sea for a patrol. The drop points were navigation aid bearings and distances or radar fixes that were extremely precise, and other than a strong surface wind that could make the passes drift off, we could be certain the drops would be on target. With squadron aircraft outbound from Saigon, day and night, at least, every nine hours or so, it was an easy mission for us to perform when tasked.

Chieu Hoi means "Open Arms." It was a South Vietnamese program which granted disgruntled Viet Cong or NVA soldiers a "safe pass" to a retraining center where they would be rehabilitated and given a financial stipend. My squadron provided the free passes day or night—as if from heaven—to the desired locations in the Rung Sat. I kept one particular pass on the day I was in the aft station of our outbound patrol, helping the crew throw out several thousand from the two boxes we had been given. In what must have been a scheduling snafu, as our aircraft was dropping the passes from low altitude, two Air Force F-5s where starting steep angle bombing runs in the area approximately beneath us. As big as we were, the pilots must have had us in plain sight, but we never heard from them, even on guard (emergency) radio frequency. They just went about their business, and we did the same.

Since we were always flying odd hours, most times we would not be able to eat regular meals. If we had a preflight between sunset and dawn, which we did many times, we would eat double C rations. As anyone can attest to who has had the pleasure, C rats gave you energy and filled your stomach—and those are the "kind" comments. The canned pecan roll was the piece de resistance of C rats and often missing from the pilfered cases we got.

In Vietnam, food was as much a key factor as bullets. Although we were billeted in the city, because of our odd hours, we ate lots of C rats, just like our buddies in the field. Since our body clocks were always confused, if we got food before a flight, we then would have to consider the tons of coffee we would be drinking during the flight to keep us pumped up. Knowing coffee was a diuretic and bowel stimulant posed a serious individual problem: How were we going to "go" before we go?

'Who shit all over my airplane'

I don't particularly like toilet humor, but my recollection of the P2V on patrol in Vietnam would not be complete without a story about the Neptune's infamous dry toilet.

Since Neptune was also thought of as king of the sea, I suppose the P2V honey bucket was his "throne." However, it was less than lavish. It was just an empty bucket attached permanently to the fuselage decking with a seat and lid. It was located in the back of the aircraft, behind the port aft observer's seat. To use it, a crewman had to line the bucket with an air sickness bag—we called them barf bags—complete his duty, fold up the bag and remove the same upon landing to the proper facility.

Well, the reality of this situation was not many ever used the bucket. The person contemplating its use would have to be "in extremis" to sit in plain view of, at least, one fellow crew member to perform his duty and then carry the bag around to dispose of it upon landing. There was absolutely no privacy. Personally, I never used it in over two-thousand flight hours in the P2V.

To make sure I never had to use the bucket, one of my preflight rituals was to do anything I could to "go" before I took off. If the flight schedule timing was right and close to my normal body clock, a couple of thick-black cups of coffee would do the trick. It was a very foreboding situation if things did not work out. Not being successful would mean constipation and an eventual dull headache.

To make matters worse, all those

in-country were required to take large yellow "horse" pills for Malaria prevention, an unpleasant ritual repeated every two weeks. Swallowing these pills guaranteed several enormous bouts of diarrhea over a time period of three to eight hours. Knowing how to time taking the pill and schedule those not-too-pleasant rush calls to the less stressful non-flying hours was a sign of having been there awhile. Woe to the newcomer who did not know that regimen of the patrol trade—which brings me to the story of a hapless lieutenant who made one cigar-chomping maintenance senior chief petty officer very unhappy.

VP-17 had replacement pilots and tactical coordinators (taccos) coming in throughout the year. Most of them were like me, "nuggets" just out of the RAG squadron, making their first tour in a fleet squadron. Others were second tour officers—those who had been in another squadron for three years, then transferred to "shore" duty for three years . . . and then back to a squadron. The officers showing up for their second tour were most often lieutenants or lieutenant commanders.

On one particular flight in my second month of continuous Market Time operations from Saigon, a newly arrived second-tour lieutenant tacco was assigned to replace someone who was sick. Though he had flown in P2V aircraft before, this was his first tour in Vietnam. Again, because of the irregular nature of day and nighttime flights, I had not met him before, even though he had been in-country three days.

As was the case during preflight, I was involved with getting the navigation charts readied for the mission and so I did not get a chance to talk with the lieutenant until we were on the flight deck together, seated side by side taxiing out to the departure end of the runway. After takeoff and a course change to drop several boxes of Chieu Hoi Psy Ops leaflets on the defoliated jungle below, I set up my navigation charts and the lieutenant warmed up the radar and tactical scope for the upcoming targets we would identify in the South China Sea. Our early morning takeoff would ensure daylight for the entire flight, a welcome change from the dark to dawn or daylight to dark flights we had been getting. After several hours, I was called up to the cockpit to relieve the copilot who had been flying from the left seat. Shortly thereafter, the plane commander called the tacco, who had taken over my navigation duties. The tacco did not respond. The commander then called the other stations and was informed the tacco had made a mad dash over the wing beam to the aft station toilet and had purged the two aft station observers out of their seats with his very persuasive thunder.

As an act of mercy for all those in the back of the aircraft, the port aft observer had opened the hinged-plexiglas waist hatch on his side and locked it in place to let in some fresh air.

At least ten minutes went by before the tacco had gained enough confidence to get on the intercom and explain himself. He apologized to the pilot for breaking the crew communications policy about leaving his seat position unannounced, but he didn't think he would have had enough time to call the cockpit and still make it back to the aft station facility.

Everything was OK now, he just didn't realize it was coming on so quickly. The plane commander, a wise old two-tour Vietnam veteran at thirty-five years of age, surmised what might have occurred and asked poignant questions. "Yup," replied the tacco, "I took one of those big Malaria pills the corpsman was giving out this morning at the flight line." Mystery solved, case closed and happy ending . . . or that's what you might have thought.

It was seven hours later when we taxied into our flight line having completed an uneventful mission. It was still daylight, and as usual, there was a senior chief in the distance standing in his khakis taking his first gander at the incoming aircraft, trying to surmise what gripes would be coming for him and his maintenance crews to repair before the aircraft was ready to fly again.

As we pulled up into the middle of the taxiway and stopped, our two aft observers dropped out of the aft belly entrance to the matting and made their way behind the whirling props to insert steel safety pins in the main landing gear. At the same time, the plane captain left his cockpit seat between the pilot and copilot, climbed down to the nose wheel tunnel, opened the accordion curtain, extended the nosewheel well entrance ladder and climbed down to the ground placing the last steel safety pin in the nose wheel before giving the pilot the signal to cut the reciprocating engines.

In an unusual move, the maintenance chief was the first person to the cockpit once the props came to a stop. He had a grin on his face and a question on his mind, though he took some time to phrase it properly. Falling back on his many years of experience in asking direct questions of his superiors while still showing the proper respect, his balanced query was: "Who shit all over my airplane . . . Sir?"

After the ground tug had been hooked up to the P2V to back it into position facing out to the taxiway, the maintenance chief and plane commander exited by the nosewheel ladder and walked back to the tail section. The chief pointed up to a considerable amount of air-dried muck sweeping diagonally from the port observer's waist window up the vertical stabilizer. Though he had never seen something like this before, in the short period of time he had to observe the aircraft as it taxied in, the chief surmised correctly what it might be.

It seems our lieutenant had been faced with a delicate predicament some seven hours before. He felt he had somewhat embarrassed himself and he had a bag to remind him of it. However, there was this tempting open waist window, a most convenient receptacle 1,000 feet above the South China Sea to deposit his package—out of sight, out of mind. As the pilot learned later, our "in-country nugget" folded the bag as tightly as possible and even found a rubber band to hold it together. He flung it out into the 160-knot slipstream, and it was gone. Now he could crawl back over the wing beam to the flight deck, take his position on the radar and plotting scope and explain himself to the pilot for leaving his station in a rush.

The bag must have exploded in the concrete force of the wind and deposited the contents in a prop-driven, swirling arc up the vertical stabilizer. Now that the culprit had been identified, the chief had only one more "sticky" question to ask. With the plane commander's concurrence, our lieutenant found himself assigned a final mission for the day. With a wash rack brush in hand, several buckets of hot soapy water, and a high check stand, he did his duty one more time.

Flying 'In country'

When not scheduled for Market Time coastal patrols, the squadron's operations department made our crews available for other missions. Coordinating with the Navy's intelligence division at MACV in Saigon, selected crews were briefed to fly straight-line tracks over the jungle, up and down the Cambodian border conducting Electronic Countermeasure (ECM) triangulations of hostile radars. It was believed at the time, the Cambodians, or the NVA with Cambodia's acquiescence, were conducting active radar surveillance of South Vietnam's airspace, just east of their own border. By using radar, the enemy could forewarn its own troops and vehicles of impending raids by either high-flying bombers or troop-carrying helicopters. From the vantage point of only 5,000 feet we could see recent bombing damage along the border, especially from the B-52s which left long black swaths across the landscape pockmarked with huge water-filled craters. This was most dramatic around the Cambodian land mass called the Parrot's Beak, named because it jutted like a beak into South Vietnam, only 30 miles from Saigon.

Because we had excellent bearing equipment for radar triangulation installed in our model P2V, our crews identified and located scores of Soviet-made equipment operating just inside Cambodia near the South Vietnamese border. These flights near the border were passive operations that we could conduct without tipping off the radar operators. If their radars were up and operating, we could analyze the signals being emitted and fix their locations. On the enemy scopes we would merely appear as a target flying close to but not violating Cambodian airspace.

Besides the ECM flights along the Cambodian border, the squadron was tasked with similar flights in the offshore areas west, south and east of Hainan Island. Radar sites on this communist Chinese island also helped the North Vietnamese by keeping track of American carrier task forces which operated in the South China Sea and Tonkin Gulf. By determining the types of radars and their locations, the Navy's intelligence community could plan countermeasures for critical operations that would blind the radars to aircraft movements.

The squadron also volunteered for tasking that could deliver critically needed parts to allied ships out at sea or in coastal areas, as part of a routine Market Time flight or a special delivery. My crew once was tasked with the delivery of a part that weighed about seventy-five pounds for a destroyer escort-sized ship at the mouth of the Cua Viet River near the Demilitarized Zone (DMZ) of North and South Vietnam. A utility boat from the vessel was launched and positioned itself about 300 yards from the ship to recover our drop. The part was packaged in a waterproof metal container that was painted orange to make it easy to spot in the sea swells.

Flying as slow as we could for our weight, we dropped the part out of the aft station belly hatch rather than the bombay from an altitude of 100 feet to the waiting auxiliary boat. The part survived the drop nicely and the utility boat easily recovered it.

Our squadron also was getting good at dropping sealed plastic tubes filled with reading material to any allied picket ship that requested them during daylight hours. Dubbed "Operation Gold Dust," our flight crews dropped three-foot-long tubes filled with the discarded magazines and paperback books which our members had read. These intellectual care packages also contained recent issues of the Stars and Stripes newspapers that were read by the military in Southeast Asia. Since most ships were on station for, at least, one month before returning to port, the Gold Dust drops were welcomed by the shipboard crews.

It may or may not have been a coincidence, or really good Viet Cong intelligence, but in mid-March 1967 as our squadron was in a turnover transition with a relieving sister squadron, a 100-foot-long steel-hulled North Vietnamese gun-running trawler was detected from the air heading directly for the Cape Batangan area of the South Vietnam coast. After making the initial identification pass at 200 feet, an aircraft from our sister squadron trailed the vessel covertly by radar and passed its location on to converging Market Time surface ships. When the trawler was hailed to surrender, it beached itself, instead. As U.S. and allied ships fired rounds along the shoreline to prevent the cargo from being unloaded, the trawler crew destroyed their vessel with a timed detonation. When boarded and inspected the next day, allied personnel could not find one useable weapon in the debris.

Island-hopping home

We were certainly proud of our sister squadron for her prowess and success so early in her six-month Market Time tour. However, our personal thoughts were about going home to Whidbey Island, a place I only got to visit once overnight on a navigation flight five months prior.

In short order, the squadron packed up all its records for surface shipment, and chartered jets to take all non-aircrew personnel back to the states. Then, it was time for all twelve P2V aircraft to be flown "Transpac," or across the Pacific, flying from island to island, "Just like back in the old days," recalled our command master chief, a veteran of World War II and Korea.

Keeping up with the navigation during Market Time was work; keeping the aircraft on course during the Transpac was a pleasure. Our initial route home would take us from Saigon to the Philippines, then to Guam. At each stop we were scheduled to rest and RON (Remain Over Night). Even though we flew at relatively low altitudes, upon approaching the island of Guam from the west, we could see the entire verdant land mass in the late afternoon sun. From the Philippines, the flight had taken us a little over eight hours at a 7,000-foot cruising altitude. I had never been to Guam before, but knowing its history, I was intrigued to see its rough-jungle topography from the air. At that time, Japanese stragglers were still being captured in the jungle twenty-two years after the end of the war. The old samurai were astonished to see modern resort hotels then in place along the same waterfronts they had defended in 1944.

From Guam we flew for eight hours on a great circle route to Wake Island, another World War II historic site. After landing and a sumptuous meal, I hiked the Heel Point and Peale Island portions of the atoll and could still find remnants of bunkers, a shore artillery piece and quite a lot of rusting invasion equipment visible in the surf. In the early evening I met some buddies who were standing at the lighted facade of the island's movie theater. In the bright light we paid our admission and walked into the building to find seats about halfway down the rows. The ceiling of the theater was lighted to look just like the night sky. After our eyes adjusted, it was the night sky; the theater being just a high perimeter foundation open to the stars with a screen in the front.

The flight from Wake to Barbers Point, Hawaii, early the next morning, was eleven hours in bright Pacific sunlight with just a few turbulent cumulus clouds to avoid by making small course changes. In a trick that only the International Date Line could play, we landed at Barbers Point on the same day as we took off from Wake Island, only earlier. So, on paper, we landed before we took off.

Even though I had a short and uneventful first tour in Vietnam, I truly appreciated the pleasures of my first visit to Hawaii. The food was great, the beaches and streets were clean, everyone spoke English, the money was greenbacks and not military script, and we didn't have to hassle or bargain with anyone for anything. Several of us rented a compact car and drove around Oahu, stopping every couple of hours at outdoor cafes for rounds of Hawaii's fancy tropical drinks.

Late the next day, our aircrews

departed before sunset to string out our twelve aircraft at twenty-minute intervals and cruising altitudes of 2,000 feet apart for the twelve hour flight to Naval Air Station Alameda, California. Since the P2V could potentially have a critical fuel shortage on this leg of the flight, the federal government continued to maintain *Ocean Station November*, a ship which floated halfway between Hawaii and the west coast to provide a navigation fix and potential rescue service for any aircraft that got into mechanical trouble or was running low on fuel. After years of obscurity, the ship was made famous by the film *The High And The Mighty*, a story by Ernest Gann about the flight of a four-engine prop passenger plane that gets into mechanical trouble about halfway to the west coast.

I was excited to call the ship that night, and envisioned a character who would answer me while being involuntarily rolled back and forth on his castered chair due to the rolling of his ship, just like the movie. It was about midnight but no one answered me or the other squadron aircraft that called long after we had passed on top. But we had a good navigation plot due to three-star fixes from the sextant, and we had *Ocean Station November* on radar approximately where it was supposed to be drifting, so we continued on into the night.

About eleven hours after takeoff,

our radar operator made out the west coast 160 miles to the east. A slight course adjustment brought us back on track to make penetration of the Air Defense Identification Zone (ADIZ) at the precise location on our flight plan and within a few minutes of the estimated time we had radioed in to the control center. The alternative to this precise requirement would have been an intercept by our own fighters and, no doubt, the pilot and myself eventually standing at attention in front of some admiral's desk saying, "Yes, sir!" and "No, sir!"

About 50 miles out from the coast and comfortably established on airways to Alameda, the pilot called back to my position.

"I've got the nav," he said, to relieve me from my duties. When I was finished with the paperwork, I crawled forward to the bow plexiglas nose—the best seat in the house—and saw the traffic-laden Golden Gate Bridge pass under our wing as we started a Ground Controlled Approach (GCA) across San Francisco Bay to Alameda.

Since I had left my car at a parking lot outside nearby Travis Air Force Base for the charter flight to the Philippines in December 1966, I parted with my crew at Alameda to retrieve it. The leisurely two-day drive up the coast to Washington state was odd. Compared with being on patrol, I felt like I was driving in slow motion!

Chapter 4

BOMBS AWAY, AND OTHER STUFF

Our six-month reprieve at Whidbey Island in April 1967 allowed us to schedule three times as many crew-training flights as had been possible during Market Time operations in Southeast Asia.

This respite from the war zone permitted the crews that had been together for some time to update their required series of qualification (qual) flights and ground evaluations that certified them as "Alpha"—able to perform any operation called upon within the broad patrol mission. Quals consisted of numerous ASW exercises, either in an electronic simulator or "on-top" a U.S. attack submarine on an ocean patrol, weapons deliveries of rockets, bombs and mines, conventional and nuclear weapons loading, and tactical communications and navigation.

Individuals also would start or complete personal qualifications in their operational specialties. In my case, I used the time during my training flights from Whidbey in 1967 to qualify as both a patrol plane third pilot and a patrol plane navigator.

If the RAG squadron was the elementary school for P2V aircrews, the fleet squadron was the finishing academy. All the academic training received and basic skills learned in earlier training came to fruition in our fleet squadron. Since hardly any ASW-training flights or operations had been scheduled while we were in Vietnam, the squadron focused most of its efforts back at home base on this primary patrol mission. The key to being able to detect, locate, identify and destroy submarines was the proper mix of knowledge, attitude, equipment and training.

To hone our academic knowledge, entire crews were scheduled into electronic trainers that simulated different ASW scenarios, the purpose being the proper use of equipment, analysis of information received, and team-coordinated tactics that allowed a weapons-delivery attack solution.

On rarer occasions, we got on-top time with a U.S. diesel or nuclear attack submarine that was inbound, outbound or transiting the west coast. These real-time scenarios were great training evolutions that added realistic, unplanned contingencies like equipment failures or turbulent weather. On-top times were mentally intense, as coarse information was continually refined over minutes or even hours to the solution that would allow us to deliver a weapon with a high-kill probability.

Destroying a submerged submarine was a mathematical solution provided by electronic sensors. To destroy or disable a submarine on the surface or as it was submerging, however, required visual skills. My introduction to weapons delivery began under the tutelage of some pilots who were in their third P2V squadron tours. They had a considerable amount of experience, the kind that did not come in manuals. Though none of them had dropped or fired a live weapon during combat, some of the more senior pilots had been trained by veterans of the Korean War. Patrol pilots in that conflict were a breed above the rest.

The United States and its allies were caught totally unprepared for North Korea's sudden attack across the 38th Parallel into the south. Without the proper military assets or manpower in place to defend against the massive onslaught, the north made rapid military gains. Incredibly, patrol crews deployed to Japan and the Philippines in the earlier models of the P2V, particularly the P2V-3, were ordered to South Korea to conduct extraordinary ground-attack missions against enemy positions. With six 20-mm fixed-nose cannons and sixteen five-inch wing rockets, the early P2Vs were formidable weapons in the hands of their neophyte "attack" crews. The necessity of the situation in Korea made the patrol crews quick studies in their new role. However, as regular attack squadrons finally began to reach the region, P2V crews were reassigned to their patrol mission, with only backup tasking for rocket attacks, photo reconnaissance, mine laying, and horizontal bombing.

Hearing these stories for the first time in the mid-1960s gave me a greater appreciation for Neptune, the patriarch, and all his progeny. Maybe I had sold him short in my earlier thinking. Now, with all these tales of courage and valor, it became clear to me that even his first son, Turtle, was ferocious, after all.

Kelly's Bombaydears

One of the most uncomplicated P2V weapons-delivery procedures was low-altitude bombing. All it required was completing the checklist, lining the aircraft up with the target, opening the P2V's huge bomb bay doors, and "pickling" the bomb release switch to drop one or more bombs, depth bombs, mines, or torpedoes. The pilot would approach from 1,000 feet and begin a power-back glide to arrive over the visual target at a minimum of 100 feet and 200-knots airspeed. Release of one or a train of weapons would occur just prior to losing sight of the target under the nose. Getting this qual was usually just a lot of fun.

It was only a little more complicated in ASW problems when the torpedo or depth bomb was dropped upon a nondescript point in the ocean

SP-2H
Neptune

(U.S. Navy)

Crew Three from VP-17 prepares their SP-2H Neptune for a Market Time patrol from Saigon in early 1967.

(Photo by author)

At Saigon, crewmen load their personal gear through an aft waist hatch.

(Photo by author)

One of the Neptune's two R-3350 reciprocating engines is checked prior to taxi.

(Photo by author)

"Zulu Echo One," an SP-2H from VP-17, flys outbound on patrol.

(U.S. Navy)

The cockpit of the SP-2H Neptune with overhead jet and recip throttles, and mixture controls.

(Photo by author)

Flying low over the South China Sea at dawn. View of the starboard wing with searchlight tip tank.

(Photo by author)

Market Time Neptune crews dropped Chieu Hoi Psy Ops leaflets over the Rung Sat Special Zone near Saigon.
(Photo by author)

A Neptune dips down to 200 feet to identify a trawler on the South China Sea.

(Photo by author)

A Soviet ship with war supplies for North Vietnam is photographed in the Gulf of Tonkin.

(U.S. Navy)

The Haiphong-bound ship is laden with construction equipment and motorized barges.

(U.S. Navy)

The SP-2H's 70-million-candlepower wing tip searchlight is apparent on this taxiing aircraft at Cam Ranh.

(U.S. Navy)

The Neptune's recip and jet engines had to receive scheduled maintenance checks during rare lulls in the flight schedule.

(U.S. Navy)

PCF "Swift" boats moored at Cam Ranh Bay. The author went on an eight-hour Market Time patrol with a Swift boat crew.

(Photo by author)

Numerous sampans were searched for arms or contraband in Cam Ranh Bay and in the nearby South China Sea.

(Photo by author)

Skipper Barry maneuvers his Swift boat to rendezvous with a larger picket ship in the South China Sea.
(Photo by author)

The Naval Air Facility at Cam Ranh Bay as viewed from 2,000 feet by a departing Market Time Neptune.
(Photo by author)

After the *Pueblo* was seized by North Korea, Neptune crews armed their aircraft with the 350-pound depth bombs seen in the foreground.

(Photo by author)

Besides depth bombs, *Pueblo* task force flight crews also loaded rockets and Mk-46 torpedoes.

(Photo by author)

The APS-20 radar enabled Neptune crews to navigate at low altitudes, and to find targets at long ranges.
(Photo by author)

This surfaced Foxtrot diesel sub was typical of the threat anticipated by *Pueblo* task force aircrews.
(Photo by author)

During a low pass on a ship, the crew aft observer takes numerous ID photos.

(U.S. Navy)

This North Vietnamese gun-running trawler was discovered positioning for a run to the coast.

(U.S. Navy)

The trawler, hiding a 12.7-mm anti-aircraft gun under its aft-deck tarp, refrained from firing upon the author's aircraft.

(U.S. Navy)

Soviet intelligence-gatherer or just a fishing boat? Photographs from Neptune crews allowed experts to analyze the antennas.

(U.S. Navy)

The bow station, the "best seat in the house." The plexiglas nose cone allowed the best visibility, but the little black handle on the lower left caused buffoonery.

(U.S. Navy)

Sonobuoys (aluminum cylinders standing upright, left center) gave later model Neptunes an all-weather ASW capability.

(U.S. Navy)

One of the last to operate. An SP-2H from Patrol Squadron 69 on duty in the Pacific Northwest until 1975.

(Photo by author)

Retired to the "boneyard." Neptunes were surplused in the late 1970s to Davis-Monthan, AZ.

(U.S. Navy)

Visiting "the TURTLE." The author (right), his copilot, CDR. Norden Cegelske, and their crew visited the Naval Aviation Museum in Pensacola, Florida, in 1981. The Truculent "ferocious" Turtle was there on display.
(Photo by CDR. Steve Ripley)

that the crew tactical coordinator had calculated to be above or just forward of a submerged submarine's course. Though it was rare, bombs also could be dropped from the eight wing-weapon stations.

The most complicated drops were mixed stores, that is, a mix of weapons in the bomb bay or on the wing stations. "Complicated," of course, is a relative term. Yet, in my recollection, it seemed that pilots of Irish descent, including myself, oftentimes had trouble remembering what weapons was where and whether the right switches had been selected. To explain this, first I'll tell Kelly's story, and then I'll tell on myself.

One of the advantages we had at Whidbey Island in 1967 was a raked-mining range. "Raked" meant that three towers were manned on the shoreline of crescent-shaped Admiralty Bay to triangulate the impact points of water-sand-filled practice bombs that simulated the precise laying of anti-shipping mines. Laying mines at the entrances to bays or harbors was a great maritime strategy, but only if the exact location of each mine was known. Thus, Neptune crews were required to qualify each year laying mines in precise patterns.

At Whidbey Island, this qual required the P2V to approach Admiralty Bay from the south at a low altitude with its bomb bay doors open. An initial point (IP) for the first drop would be determined by the radar operator. The subsequent simulated mines would be dropped at timed intervals computed on the aircraft's ground speed. The rake station observers would visually triangulate each practice bomb's explosive-white tail plume and radio the crew a "hit" or "miss" result.

From what I recall, my friend Kelly had one of those mixed loads on board his aircraft that day. Half of his bomb bay was loaded with eight practice bombs for two qual attempts and the other side was loaded with a empty 350-gallon aviation fuel-tank bladder that measured seven-feet long, three-feet tall and three-feet wide. The tank, one of two usually installed to give the P2V the range it needed for a Transpac, was connected to bomb racks so it could be jettisoned in case of an emergency. Getting rid of both fuel bladders in an emergency would immediately relieve the aircraft of 4,200 pounds of weight.

But getting back to the story: Kelly made one run that was evidently "OK" but could have been better. With the bomb bay stores selector switch now repositioned presumably on the correct stations to drop the next four practice bombs, Kelly made his precision run to place what turned out to be the largest mine ever witnessed by the rake station crews and the nearby salmon fishermen who usually drifted lackadaisically on the edge of the range. The empty fuel bladder hit the water with a huge splash and bounced back up somewhat before coming to rest floating in the bay. The rake station operators reported the drop was right on target—a hit! But unfortunately, the precision of the big "simulated mine" was compromised as it drifted slowly off its mark toward the shoreline.

Being a typical Irishman who can feel guilty about anything, Kelly owed up to the flub and adopted a crew patch which depicted an old biplane in level flight dropping a huge black fuel tank from its belly. His crew, quick to realize what others might try to make of the incident, defused the situation by adopting "Kelly's Bombaydears" as their proud moniker.

'I got the quals'

What goes around, comes around. Eight years later as a P2V patrol plane commander in a reserve patrol squadron, I found it tough to get any qual flight in the typical one day per month we were scheduled to fly as a crew. There were many times when just one flight qualification took two or more months to complete because we lacked an integral crew or because the aircraft or weather did not cooperate. However, on a particular flight to requalify for rockets and bombs, I was all pumped up because I finally had all of my crew together.

We flew out to a restricted area

over the Pacific Ocean and descended to 1,000 feet above the waves where the ordnanceman dropped one long-burning smoke signal from the aft station. We would use this floating smoke as a simulated target for both the bombs and the rockets.

With the bombing checklist complete and ships clear of the area, I opened the bomb bay doors and descended rapidly from 1,000 feet to a straight-in approach on the target smoke at 200 feet and 200 knots. Just before the smoke went under the nose of the aircraft, I pressed the bomb-release switch. Nothing happened.

The qual observer looking in the bomb bay from the bomb bay viewing port in the radio station called with the news—none of the bombs had dropped. So we tried a second time after double-checking all the proper switches. Again, nothing.

Not wanting to waste time, I chose to climb to 2,500 feet to begin the rocket-qual portion of the flight. We would fire the fourteen rockets that were attached in two rocket pods, one pod mounted on each wing. This was always an exciting evolution and everyone on the crew looked forward to it, like anticipating an exhilarating roller coaster ride.

The Neptune as an air-to-surface rocket-attack platform was just unbelievable. The SP-2H models were as big as modern DC-9s. Just imagine an aircraft that large descending rapidly from a low altitude in a steep dive to fire rockets be-

ROCKET PATTERN

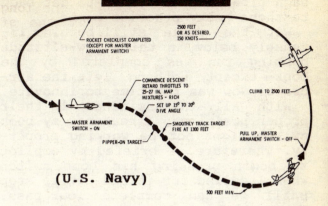

(U.S. Navy)

fore recovering at only 500 feet. Though I had qualified in rockets many times since my initial introduction in 1967, it still was a thrill to nose over such a large aircraft and point it down with the gunsight aimed at a target.

Passing through 1,300 feet, the first rocket to fly from the aircraft was for effect. Once its impact was observed, a forceful adjustment—close to manhandling the aircraft's pitch or roll—would be necessary to walk-fire three or four more rockets to the target before pulling steadily back on the yoke to affect a pullup.

As thrilling as it was to fire the 2.75-inch rockets, I understood from reading I had done at the time, it was child's play in comparison with the formidable 5-inch rockets that earlier P2V crews had as firepower. Nevertheless, the thrill was not gone and two more passes on the smoke below us resulted in a qual each time. Now we needed to get back to those pesky practice bombs.

With the smoke still burning intensely below, a third low-altitude bombing run was completed by the book—except nothing left the aircraft. Now was the time to innovate.

With all the switches in their proper positions, I reasoned my bomb switch might not be working properly. Therefore, I briefed my copilot to begin pressing his bomb switch when I called for it and not to stop until we had completed our pass. Long before the target smoke went under the nose, I called for the copilot to begin depressing his bomb switch. In this way, if the bombs went at all, they would straddle the target and result in a qual.

"Bombs away" was the sweet response from the bomb bay window observer. This was only a little odd since the call came several seconds after the copilot began to depress his release switch.

"We just dropped the rocket pods, too," added one of the aft station observers.

Whoops! I had no idea why the pods dropped off the wings, but thank God, they fell harmlessly into the ocean below without the rockets in them.

In the peacetime training status of late 1975, I knew, rightfully so, that I would have a lot of explaining to do. Even the "innovation" that one might have used in a wartime scenario to sink a submarine by any means possible would probably not have included rocket pods. So, I need not daydream about that as an excuse.

With a definite somber feeling—I knew I had screwed up in some way—I flew back to base where I wrote up an ordnance gripe for the technicians to investigate. I knew the next morning I was going to have to face the safety officer to explain why two perfectly-good rocket pods inadvertently left the aircraft.

Early the next day, the petty officer technician from ordnance who worked on the maintenance gripe told me the weapon station selector switch in my previous day's aircraft had been defective.

"Whew!" not a total screw up. I felt somewhat relieved. An internal set screw had backed out allowing the rotary-wafer electrical contacts to run four stations ahead of what had been selected and visible in the cockpit. Shortly thereafter things were looking even brighter as the flight observer gave me the paperwork to complete both a rocket and bomb qual. Since two of our bombs hit within a couple of feet of the target smoke, nothing in the rules disqualified me for throwing out a little extra iron into the ocean.

With my report in hand, I sought out the safety officer. He had already heard about the inadvertent ordnance drop. He was not happy.

As a civilian attorney who was in the grooming stage to be the next executive officer and then commanding officer of this reserve patrol squadron, he reviewed my report initially with skepticism and dread. It was his job to review all incidents to uncover the causes, and institute procedures or policies that would preclude them from happening again. But, safety matters in squadrons seemingly always reflected upon the leadership, and in that additional context, I assumed he was also intent to see if any of my aberrant, innovative behavior might be pointed in his direction.

With the experience of a prosecutor, he sat me on a chair situated in the middle of his office. In this way, he had the room to pace back and forth in long strides for effect, puffing from time to time and pointing the stem of his pipe to underscore his poignant questions. He only began to relax when he realized I had tried several times to go exactly by the book, and no one was physically hurt or had their property destroyed in the matter. He wouldn't have to write a safety report that was critical of the command because of me.

That didn't mean I was off the hook. He kept it professional—never stooping to a personal attack—but he chewed me up one side and down the other. After five minutes of this, his parting words to me were: "Once you saw that it didn't work by the book, you should have stopped right there and come back to base."

As I left his office, somewhat flushed for the short harangue that I deserved, I kept on hearing his words in my ears: "You should have stopped .. ." Though I knew he was right and I was wrong, as I got to the hallway, I could not help but to fantasize and mouth what might have been a brilliant comeback: "But, I got the quals!"

Sniff around like a beagle

Believe it or not, my SP-2H model Neptune was equipped to sniff around the oceans of the world like a beagle for the scent of a snorkeling diesel submarine. One of our annual quals in 1967 was an exercise to follow an exhaust trail, presumably from a submerged diesel submarine that would be transiting an area using its snorkel system. The snorkel was developed by the Dutch before World War II but perfected by Nazi Germany to allow its submarines to cruise underwater on their long-range diesel engines, rather than on their limited batteries. The snorkel intake and exhaust tubes would be the only portion of the submarine exposed during transit, making it less likely to be spotted visually or by radar.

In the 1960s, with half of the world's submarines still using diesel power, the AN/ASR-3 system was potentially useful. To obtain a qual on what we called the "Sniffer" system, we more often than not had to find a particularly smoky freighter that was alone at sea; or being in the Northwest, a particularly smoldering lumber or paper mill. Patrol aircraft that came after the P2V were not equipped with Sniffer since the Environmental Protection Agency had all but eliminated our potential training targets.

A Sniffer scoop mounted on top of the aircraft's nose would monitor the air during a patrol. Making the assumption that detected fumes were drifting in the wind, a pilot would fly the aircraft back and forth across and into the prevailing wind, narrowing the source of the combustion exhaust until a visual or radar sighting was made. This system never proved fruitful for any crew I was in, but I understand it worked well, at least, once during the Cuban Missile Crisis of 1963 in initially detecting a transiting Soviet-block submarine.

Smile, look at the birdie

Photoflash was another unique system built into the P2V to obtain low-level nighttime photographs of darkened targets on the ocean. In the days before low-level-light television or sniper scopes, the Navy concocted this system to take nighttime photographs of snorkeling submarines or small surface targets from an altitude of only 300 feet. It was meant to work like early photographers who used flash powder in a tray to provide sufficient light for an image.

It was a great concept and I guess a viable tool if you needed it. However, more often than not, it just caused a lot of havoc and sleepless nights for the birds nesting on the islands or rock pinnacles that were buzzed by our crews looking to obtain a qual. The joke was that no surface ship would allow us to overfly them at night and shoot photoflash cartridge bursts at them. The birds, on the other hand, had no congressmen to represent them.

The low-level star bursts timed only seconds apart to synchronize with a fuselage-mounted camera must have been very disconcerting for man and beast. At least one manual warned that training flights would only be scheduled over "designated target areas," but in no case would "cartridges be used over friendly inhabited areas."

Luckily, we were never tasked to use the photoflash system operationally. I couldn't imagine any target, friend or foe, not firing back at us once we made a pass. Nevertheless, in 1967 we were required to be proficient in its use and, thus, our squadron obtained quals at night making radar and photoflash passes on the disenfranchised birds who inhabited nearby Smith Island and some of the rock pinnacles off the western shore of the Olympic Peninsula.

The blood-red ocean

One of the operational missions we were tasked to fly once a week from our home base was the surveillance of both the Soviet fishing and whaling fleets that operated separately off the coasts of Oregon and Washington. From the spring through the fall of every year, one or two Soviet fishing fleets of twenty or so trawlers and a "mother" factory ship operated right up to the twelve-mile territorial limit of the United States. We were sent out to locate and chart the areas in which they fished, take photographs of their operations and potentially identify any intelligence-gathering trawlers they had on site posing as a fishing vessel. By treaty, the Soviets were limited to fishing for hake and not salmon, but there was no way for us to be able to determine this from the air. Thus, we turned over all the photographs we took of their catches to our squadron intelligence officer who sent them on to Washington, D.C. for closer analysis by treaty monitors.

Every once and a while, we would spot a relatively clean fishing trawler with a lot of sophisticated antennas installed on the superstructure or rigging. These, we suspected, were the perfunctory "AGI" or intelligence-gathering trawlers the Soviets would send out with the fishing fleets to gather information on our coastal communications and submarine transits.

For these patrols to be of any use to the intelligence community, it was important for us to get out timely position and activity reports on these foreign fleets. To ensure good communications so far from the coastline, our radio operator would spool out a heavy-gage cooper wire antenna up to 215 feet behind the aircraft in flight. The antenna had a weighted conical-shaped end that ensured it would trail behind the aircraft in the slip-stream.

On my last fishing and whaling fleet patrol of 1967, a month before we were to deploy back to the Philippines and Vietnam, my crew headed directly west several hundred miles from the northwestern tip of the Olympic Peninsula to begin a search pattern. We were only forty-five minutes into our ocean search when our radar called out three medium-sized targets 100 miles to the southwest. With no other blips showing on radar, we departed our prescribed search pattern and flew directly to the targets.

"Oh, my God, look at that," exclaimed the plane commander, as the targets came into view twenty minutes later. Since I was back on the flight deck and working as navigator, I had to wait until we marked on-top two of the three targets to fix their position, before I could leave my station to see why the pilot had made such a disconcerting comment.

He wasn't understating his shock

and surprise. It was a sight no one would forget in a lifetime. I hadn't considered myself much of a conservationist up to that point, but the sight of a blood-red ocean around two floating whale carcasses gave me a foreboding feeling.

Something was just not right with the world after viewing such unnecessary carnage. The maroon-colored blood from the whales totally dominated the otherwise deep blue-green color of the Pacific in an irregular circle around a huge drifting Soviet factory ship and smaller whaler.

A second whaler was underway only a mile away and in hot pursuit of a pod of whales, possibly the same group that had produced the first two kills. We could not tell what species of whale the Soviets had killed, so we swooped down many times to take enough photos for others to be able to tell. It was impossible to be detached from this happenstance—we all felt sickened by the scene we had observed. If we could have stopped it, I think we would have tried, but, of course, that was impossible.

We covered the remainder of our whaling-surveillance area without further contacts, and somberly changed course to begin a search for the Soviet fishing fleets somewhere to the southeast and closer to the coast.

How low did you go?

A large number of smaller targets

in the vicinity of one large radar blip was a giveaway to the position of one of the Soviet fishing fleets. A small course correction brought us in thirty minutes to the frenzied activity of numerous small trawlers dropping their nets and bringing their catches to a nearby factory ship. We found this flotilla only 70 miles northwest of the mouth of the Columbia River, the largest salmon fishery on the U.S. West Coast. Yet, these ships were bound by treaty to be fishing only for hake.

We went about our photo and visual identifications of all the ships including one that looked like an AGI. Not having the ability to step out and board the vessel, and it being in international waters, anyway, we concentrated on this one vessel, which we thought might be a bad guy. Considering we weren't happy with the Soviets, in general, that day, we might have pressed harder that afternoon to get exceptionally-clear intelligence photos.

When we were finished with this fleet, we continued our search pattern to the south looking for a possible second fishing fleet, but nine hours into our flight, we ended our track off the Oregon coast without finding it. We assumed from the lack of contacts, it probably had departed for Siberia sometime since the last patrol.

About thirty minutes from Whidbey on our airways return flight, the radio operator called the plane commander with an interesting little tidbit for the maintenance gripe sheet. About 150 feet of the trailing-wire antenna and its weighted end were missing. The radioman had stopped using the antenna for long-distance communications when the aircraft had marked on-top the fishing fleet, and only now had begun to try to reel it in.

"Just how low did you go on that AGI?" the radioman asked, already assuming he knew the answer.

We might have lost our trailing-wire antenna wrapped around the ship's rigging, but if we did, we presumed a bad guy might not be showing up at a U.S. port to lodge a protest.

Our logic turned out to be pretty good that day because we never heard about a complaint, or a missing trailing-wire antenna turned in at any port district lost and found office.

The episodes with the Soviet whaling and fishing fleets highlighted the end of my crew's six month "rest" period back in the states. By the beginning of the next month, we would be back in Vietnam.

Chapter 5

VIETNAM, THE TEMPO INCREASES

It was obvious in the first weeks of arriving back in Vietnam that the tempo of operations had significantly increased. We were now located at the expanded air base at Cam Ranh Bay and sharing the Market Time commitment with two other patrol squadrons. The new strategy was to search the seaborne arms-infiltration routes more often, and to be available for other special operations.

Our return trip of island-hopping westbound over the Pacific had been idyllic: Low head winds, strong tail winds, no mechanical problems, beautiful little cumulus clouds dispersed artistically for effect, and a verbal response from the man on *Ocean Station November*—just like the movie, *The High and the Mighty*.

We, again, established our headquarters and maintenance base at Sangley Point in the Philippines and sent six aircraft and crews to Vietnam to begin round the clock patrols. The Cam Ranh Peninsula on the central coast looked like a huge sand dune from the air that protected a twelve-mile-long bay from the South China Sea. At the air base on the north end of the peninsula, one long concrete runway and a shorter parallel runway made of solid metal mats were situated to take advantage of the consistent strong winds that blew from the northeast. A really new experience was taking off on the metal-mat runway in a fully-loaded P2V. It was akin to driving a mile through a mall parking lot at an ever increasing velocity and hitting every speed bump along the way. It made such a racket, I always thought the landing gear was going to shear off before I could ease back on the yoke and get the heavy Neptune into the air.

Cam Ranh Air Base was quite a nice place, all modern facilities and good food. Most appreciatively, the C rations of the past were gone, replaced by the luxury of box lunches or meals prepared by a flight galley. We also had a separate flight line at the new Naval Air Facility (NAF) on the west side of the parallel runways, opposite the Air Force squadron and service areas.

Anyone who was at Cam Ranh can remember the sand. For the six months I was there off and on during my second tour, when the wind blew greater than twenty knots—which it did often—those of us who lived there had sand in our eyes, sand in our teeth, sand in our ears, sand in our hair . . . and sand in other places.

Sunrise zombies

Unlike my first Vietnam tour, the

missions starting in late 1967 involved more flights but less time in the air per mission. With the fifteen- to twenty-hour ground times we had between flights, our body clocks quickly became really screwed up. Oftentimes, though we planned to sleep six to eight hours during the day before beginning a dusk preflight, all we did was toss and turn and fret about the lack of sleep we were getting.

Our worst flight evolutions were those that found us still flying at sunrise with two hours to go on a nine-hour patrol. It was just impossible to stay awake during those slow tropical sunrises that sapped the last bit of energy out of us when we were already tired, hot, and probably terribly dehydrated. On more than one occasion when I was on the navigation table and having trouble staying awake myself, I would call to the cockpit with a new heading change, and not get an answer. During those incidents we probably had been flying on shaky Iron Mike—the auto pilot—at an altitude of only 500 to 1,000 feet between the targets we were investigating. At that altitude it would have taken only seconds for us to fly sleepily into the sea below.

Not that I was any better. Once or twice during this tour, when it was my turn to fly in the left cockpit seat, I confessed I could not keep my eyes open any longer against the glare and intensity of the rising sun.

"Could you guys cover me for five minutes? I've got to close my eyes," I would beg the copilot and plane captain. With their groggy nod of acquiescence, I would let myself go, falling quickly into a deep zombie-like state that sounds could not penetrate . . . but silence could. It was the silence of no radio traffic or crew communications, most times, that snapped me out of my trance and back into a cockpit where everyone was zonked . . . except Iron Mike, who had just enough electrons in his system to keep him unerringly flying us straight into a huge emerging orb.

Skyscraper out of the darkness

One of our first Market Time flights after returning to Vietnam was a night-ocean search using our 70-million candlepower carbon-arc searchlight. Mounted in the forward section of the starboard (right) wing tip fuel tank, the searchlight produced a bright, narrow and directional light source that we could use to illuminate and identify ships in the dark.

Our Market Time protocol for night searches was to plot all radar targets within our immediate range and to discard those "squawking" the appropriate electronic IFF (Identification Friend or Foe) codes for that time period.

A valid squawk meant the target we saw highlighted on our radar screen was a Market Time picket ship or allied military vessel. All the other targets we would fly over at a minimum of 200 feet to inspect and hopefully identify. If we were coming in on a target that had no IFF code showing on radar or was cruising without its mast or superstructure lights on, the bow observer would flash a Morse light code with his portable Aldis lamp. Receiving the correct blinker in reply, we would assume the vessel was a friendly ship and move on to the next radar target to investigate.

If our darkened quarry would not or could not respond with the proper signal for the night, the copilot, who had directional control of the searchlight, would light off the target. Once illuminated, the target could usually be identified by either the bow or aft observer. It was a serious matter for us to come upon a darkened target at night, for unless it was one of our own military vessels waiting in ambush, it more than likely was a target that did not want to be found or followed.

With the tempo of operations increasing all round, on many of our patrols we were given coordinates of areas to remain clear of while on our coastal surveillance tracks. To the best of my recollection, this often meant a scheduled B-52 bombing mission, a seaborne attack being planned or raids by Navy Seals or helicopter gunships.

On one such "routine" patrol, we

were given coordinates to avoid off the My Tho River Delta, part of the greater Mekong. Due to the security maxim of only giving detailed information to the participants, we were only told it was a "big operation" and to stay outside the coordinates given. No big deal, we could do that.

About 3 A.M. at the tail end of our patrol on what crews would call a "black-ass night," our radar operator called out a large, single target to the northwest, range 60 miles, not squawking an IFF. With no other targets on his screen for 100 miles except a few "friendlies" squawking the appropriate IFF, we turned directly to this contact. I had been in the copilot's seat, having been relieved of my navigation duties by the crew tacco. For the two hours I had been sitting as copilot, we had made low passes on lighted ships, mostly large cargo ships in designated shipping lanes, and on a few darkened targets that had flashed back the appropriate blinker reply to the bow observer.

The one time I used the searchlight had been on a moderate-sized wooden junk that we could not identify otherwise except by illuminating it with the powerful beam. The positions, courses and speeds of all these and previous contacts we had sent out by radio to the Market Time control center where they were plotted and tracked.

Still 40 miles out and closing,

the tacco informed the plane commander that the target was situated 10 miles outside the coordinates of the big operation and might be a freighter heading for the Saigon River. At about five miles out, the plane commander and I strained to see out the cockpit windshield, anticipating we would see lights from a large target. With still no visual sighting, the pilot told the bow observer to begin flashing that night's code on his Aldis lamp.

Though it was early in the morning, the adrenalin perked us up and out of our grogginess when the plane commander ordered everyone immediately to their stations for an identification run on a darkened target at two miles. Our target was not answering our blinker challenge.

With no haze to obscure us from seeing lights, if there had been any, and no IFF showing on radar, the pilot ordered the radar operator to go sector search, and asked me to standby the searchlight. Approaching at 180 knots and 200 feet altitude above the water, the plane commander called for the searchlight.

Out of the darkness loomed the mass of a steel skyscraper with its pillars, windows and antennas rushing towards us at an incredible speed. Only the plane commander's rapid instincts, jerking us to the left in a steep climbing turn kept us from flying into the high antennas of this huge metal-gray apparition.

"Turn the searchlight off," the

pilot barked at me, after he caught his breath. Knowing the procedure, I reminded him the arc had to remain lighted for another couple of seconds or the searchlight carbons would fuse together. Thus, our encounter then became somewhat of a Hollywood premier or grand opening during our climb to altitude.

With the searchlight off and the aircraft at 2,000 feet circling the target below, the plane commander began to take stock of what had just happened. He called for the radar to begin a circular search again and get a good fix of our position and the skyscraper-sized U.S. helicopter carrier we had just encountered seconds before.

There is a certain amount of dread that goes with military aviation. My plane commander had a definite bout of it that night. The dread of coming within seconds of buying the farm—and taking the crew along, and the dread of impacting a ship which was nearly as high as the altitude we were flying. To a lesser degree, only because anything short of death and destruction is minor, the dread of having screwed up also came across all our minds.

Were we inside or outside the zone the briefer warned us to avoid? Check and double check. While we were thinking out our individual parts in this play and collectively covering our butt with several good radar fixes, our natural defense mechanism began to kick in.

Our target LPH ship (Landing Platform Helicopter), about half the size of a standard aircraft carrier, had not been squawking an IFF code, had not answered our bow Aldis lamp challenge and had not tried to contact us on guard or Market Time frequency when we were inbound. The more we thought about it, the more bizarre it seemed to us. We probably caused the ship to replace every outside watch station after we assuredly blinded them all with our 70-million-candlepower pass. Yet, the ship still had not tried to contact us.

We orbited their position for about four minutes, but just to be safe—in case we were the ones that screwed up—the plane commander chose to leave well enough alone and proceed on our track. Since our gray ghost was not making headway, a report on his static position to our debriefing officer might sooner or later uncover his identity and purpose.

We never found out the name or mission of the ship we blinded that night. For whatever reason, the LPH chose not to report his "daylight" encounter with us in the predawn, and we were satisfied we had been in the proper search area, flying by the proper protocol.

As crews do, we told the story of this phantom ship many times, and the tale got better with every telling. In today's vernacular our story might have gone something like this:

We found a target as big as a skyscraper floating in the South China Sea. It must have been a surprise party for us, because "*the lights were out, but everyone was at home.*"

Within a month of our searchlight encounter with the LPH, patrol aircraft were urged to use para-flares instead of the searchlight to identify darkened targets. In that way, aircraft could launch flares above a target and identify it while remaining at a safe altitude and out of sight in the darkness.

Operating in the Tonkin Gulf

One of the new operations we were assigned during our 1967-68 deployment was assisting the ships of the carrier task force in the Gulf of Tonkin to identify nighttime surface targets in their vicinity. Assigned to "Red Crown," the northern-most ship in the gulf, we would mark on-top the ship's red light, which could only be seen from above, and fly outbound without any of our aircraft lights on to investigate the hundreds of junks, sampans, fishing trawlers and freighters that plied the waters at night. Being usually no more than 50 miles from our "playmate" on any one of our sweeps, we could talk instantaneously to the ship on a "covered" or secure voice radio frequency.

These six- to seven-hour missions, scheduled almost exclusively for the dark hours, gave the carrier and its screening ships warning of any potential threats against them by North Vietnamese warships that might try to hide among the legitimate traffic. The majority of these targets, however, were fishing junks that were enroute to or returning from fishing grounds. If we found a suspicious target, usually a steel-hulled vessel, our playmate would dispatch a warship in the picket line to investigate it.

Though the Soviet Union was not a combatant in the Vietnam Conflict, it had a stake in helping the North Vietnamese maintain their power in the region. One of the services the Soviets provided the North Vietnamese was the locations and status of allied warships in the gulf. Wherever the task force was cruising, a Soviet AGI was surely following. On several occasions in 1968, we would report the presence of the Soviet AGI, *Amphemeter*, to our control ship as one of the steel-hulled contacts in his vicinity. The AGI would cruise with its running lights on, so we would have no reason to use our searchlight or paraflares to identify it. But in a twist, since we were not using our aircraft lights—to keep ourselves from being a small-arms target for the junks— the *Amphemeter* crew would, on most occasions, aim their powerful shipboard searchlight at our aircraft to blind us as we flew overhead.

Sister squadron loses aircraft

The dangers inherent in the Market Time patrol mission were brought home in January 1968 by the loss of a P-3 Orion surveillance aircraft and its entire crew. The aircraft belonged to a Navy patrol squadron based in U Taphao, Thailand, but conducting Market Time missions in the southern sector of South Vietnam. We considered the unit a "sister" squadron because we flew the same mission under the same operational commander.

The aircraft had been lost in the Gulf of Thailand off the South Vietnamese island of Phu Quoc while conducting a Market Time patrol. My squadron had operated in that same sector the year before without being challenged by any Cambodian gunboats in the demarcation area north of Phu Quoc that bordered the Cambodian sea frontier. However, when VP-17 was tasked to help look for survivors, we were told to be vigilant. The unarmed aircraft reportedly had been hit by gunfire from one or more Cambodian gunboats, and crashed soon thereafter in the waters adjacent to the South Vietnamese island.

No retaliatory action was taken by the United States against Cambodia for the loss of the aircraft and crew. Unfortunately, history was to repeat itself in a short period of time.

Three months later, I was working alone at the Cam Ranh Coastal Patrol Center about dinner time when I got an unusual telephone call. As duty watch officer, I had sent my enlisted personnel to the chow hall for their evening meal and was reading through the message boards for the third time that day when I got a call on the red phone from a captain. I don't recall who he was, but considering he was calling me on the secure line from Market Time headquarters, I took it he was someone important.

He asked me somewhat innocuously if I would check a latitude and longitude position to see where it fell on our large Market Time wall chart. Even though it was 1968, our charts were seriously lacking in many respects. The best I could tell the captain was the position he gave me appeared to be just north of Phu Quoc Island, in the waters between South Vietnam and southwestern Cambodia.

Not being happy with my answer, he asked me to further check the same position on one of my airways navigation charts. Using a plotter and dividers, I was surprised the position was exactly on the line—as fine as a needle point can be—that divided Vietnamese and Cambodian airspace. With this information, my caller gave a hushed "Thank you" and ended the conversation.

It was within an hour of the telephone conversation that the message center brought in an alert communications that described the downing of another P-3 Orion by gunfire from a Cambodian patrol boat in the area I had described to the caller. The message stated there were no known survivors among the twelve crew members. Later I was to learn that the aircraft and crews lost in both January and April were from the same squadron. What a terrible loss.

Four days later in the Southeast Asian edition of the Stars and Stripes, the U.S. Military Command in Vietnam confirmed that a P-3 had been lost earlier in the week after the crew radioed being "hit by antiaircraft fire." The newspaper confirmed, there had been no survivors, though two bodies had been recovered from the water. The article went on to say the aircraft crashed five miles south of Phu Quoc Island but had been hit "while patrolling the area between the island and the mainland."

The UPI (United Press International) reported Rep. Mendel Rivers, chairman of the House Armed Services Committee, said he had information that "a Cambodian PT boat had shot down a Navy patrol plane," but he declined to say where he got the information.

"We should send ships into Cambodian waters and sink every Cambodian naval vessel and let the chips fall where they may," Rivers concluded in the news article.

Again, no retaliatory action was taken against "neutral" Cambodia.

Operation 'San Magoo'

During wartime, certain commodities historically have become universal mediums of exchange because they are in such great demand. Cigarettes, chocolate and nylons are just a few that come immediately to mind from earlier wars.

Vietnam was a well-supplied conflict, but it was a little overstocked at times with certain items. I recall on one visit to the base exchange at Cam Ranh, I found every imaginable type of olive produced in the world. A super freighter full of olives must have arrived in Vung Tau or Saigon and the exchange at Cam Ranh had panicked in ordering, thinking it would run out before the end of the war. There must have been fifteen varieties of olives in two-hundred full cases in the middle of the store. I also must have panicked because by the time I left the base five months later, I still had ten jars of pimento and almond-stuffed olives to leave to whoever was going to occupy my bunk room.

In Vietnam, one of the rarest commodities was good beer. Not that beer didn't make its way to Vietnam in great quantity, but the word on the street and in the jungles was American beer had formaldehyde in it to keep it from spoiling in the hot holds of inbound ships.

Whether that was true or not, the chemical additive also was blamed for the tens of thousands of headaches that the allies were incurring every day—since everyone had already discounted the "quantity" factor of drinking beer.

The Vietnamese beer called Tiger was bad and mercifully hard to get. "Ba Moui Ba" or 33 was just as bad but easier to find. The Dutch beer "Heineken" was outstanding but impossible to get in the quantities needed for my squadron's Vietnam operation.

Into this apparent void came a simple but coordinated-marketing opportunity that would rival the best Navy "Cumshaw" operation. Cumshaw is an unofficial Navy term for the undocumented procurement of what you desperately need or want for your squadron mates by "trading"—in the loosest sense of the word—or by whatever other means necessary.

In the case of my squadron, it was an up front, above board operation of supply and demand: The Philippines had great San Miguel Beer, and Vietnam wanted it. No government funds were used, but Uncle Sam helped out a little with the transportation. Since squadron aircraft and crews were repositioning to our Philippine maintenance base every three to four weeks, and then returning to Vietnam by flying OSAP (Ocean Surveillance Patrols) missions by the Chinese-occupied Paracel Islands, the maintenance department could put on a "few extra pounds" in bomb bay luggage racks and on the bomb bay doors.

"San Magoo," which we called the

premium Philippine beer, was brewed in Manila just 15 miles from our Sangley Point maintenance base. My figures may not be totally correct, but I believe our chiefs' mess bought each case of twenty-four bottles for four dollars, shipped about fifty cases on each P2V flight returning to Vietnam to completely fill our squadron's own needs . . . and had enough left over to barter for what it wanted. All of our personnel in-country, for example, were issued new combat boots—which we couldn't get from the Navy, but easily from "other sources."

On my last repositioning flight from the Philippines to Cam Ranh Bay in 1968, I was now a qualified co-pilot and not required to sit on the navigation table. In this new capacity, I was more aware of the weight of the additional fifty or so cases of San Magoo that was on board in the bomb bay but knew it would not be a problem for our short eight-hour flight. After making an extensive visual surveillance of all the Paracel Islands, looking for North Vietnamese trawlers that might be replenishing for a run to the South Vietnamese coast, we headed southwest in a surface search track that would bring us directly to Cam Ranh Bay.

We checked out just a few more contacts after leaving the Paracel Islands, so the remainder of our trip took us only four hours. After taxiing into our flight line, we could see a line of vehicles and its manpower waiting anxiously for our arrival. They were biding their time until our big R-3350 recips could be "chopped" and the huge props idle down to a complete stop. Then the throng converged on us, gathering around the bomb bay doors, which we had opened slowly using the back up emergency system.

At least six people in two trucks rapidly unloaded the cases of Magoo for transportation to the mess locker about a quarter of a mile away. After my crew finished its post-flight checks and was set to depart for the debriefing office, we found the bomb bay empty and ourselves standing conspicuously alone, way out on the flight line.

Priorities being what they were, we hoisted our heavy gear on our backs and began a long walk in the hot sun.

Boarding sampans

Not just content with flying my Market Time patrols, I took advantage of a standing offer from our salt-water Navy counterparts to go on an eight-hour waterborne mission that would board sampans to look for arms or contraband.

As my crew's junior officer, I had just come off of a nighttime watch at Cam Ranh and would not be committed to fly for another fifteen hours. Since I had seen the beach many times and did not care to go to sleep, I called the naval base at the south end of the Cam Ranh Peninsula to see if I could sign on for a waterborne patrol. As luck would have it, if I could be down at the base in two hours, I could join the crew of a "Swift" boat that was going out into the bay and coastal area for a daylight patrol to inspect or board fishing boats and sampans.

With a few gooey candy bars in my pockets, my olive drab uniform and jungle boots on, and a camera slung around my shoulder, I hitched a ride on a sandy road that left the Air Force defense perimeter for the naval base in the south. Twenty minutes later, I introduced myself to Barry, a lieutenant junior-grade like me, who would be the skipper for the patrol. He was an unusual blackshoe (term means shipboard, as opposed to aviators, who wear brown shoes) skipper, however, in that he also wore the gold wings of a naval aviator.

He was busy preparing for his launch, but explained to me as I shadowed him that he had been an A-4 Skyhawk pilot at one time. After his third-forced cockpit ejection in the aircraft—once earlier in the training command—his superiors asked him if he wanted to continue to chance fate. Strongly indicating he still wanted to be in the fight, he asked his detailer for an assignment to Swift boats. Now he was seeing the war from a different perspective.

The mission for this day patrol

would be an initial sweep of all the Vietnamese sampans and junks around the base, a further search and possible boardings around the south end of the bay and a cursory search a short distance outside the bay to meet up with a larger gunboat doing picket duty in the South China Sea.

My fifty-foot aluminum hull, shallow draft, fast patrol boat, designated as a PCF, was moored to another craft on the end of the pier. I only had a short wait before the crew came on board to depart.

After Barry maneuvered the boat away from the pier and into the mouth of the bay, he cruised west and then north into the bay visually checking boat traffic coming and going into a village on the western shoreline of the peninsula. A petty officer showed me the over-and-under .50-caliber machine gun/81-mm mortar mounted on the aft deck of the PCF. This was the vessel's most formidable weapon but it would not be used unless there was a suspicious boat to board or, of course, a firefight. On occasion, he said, Swift boats on patrol would take small arms fire from the shoreline when in an unsecured area.

When the PCF was preparing to board a junk or sampan, the crew would be armed with M-16s, but only flaunt them, if necessary, to obtain cooperation. My job during the boarding evolutions, he said, was to stand in the pilot house or outside opposite the boarding-party side to observe and stay out of the way. This seemed reasonable to me considering they rightfully did not offer me a weapon for my personal protection. I also supposed the worst case scenario would have been to jump ship and start swimming away if a close-in fire fight erupted. That probably wouldn't be necessary, the crewman assured me with a smile.

In short order we found two seemingly abandoned and drifting sampans which the crew chose not to physically investigate or take in tow, in case one or both of them had been bobby-trapped. Several other small sampans in the southern part of the bay were visually checked but not boarded. About four hours into our patrol, as we were cruising eastbound for the mouth of the bay, Barry sighted a medium-sized, canopied sampan in the distance. He alerted the crew that he wanted to inspect this craft, and changed course to intercept it.

The crew quietly went about the call to general quarters, putting on flak vests and loading their M-16s. Having been through this drill hundreds of times, they were ready for boarding when the hail was given. A crew member who spoke just enough of the sing-song Vietnamese language boarded after the thirty-foot stubby sampan was lashed to the port side of the Swift boat. We lost sight of the petty officer as he started searching the sampan for weapons or war contraband.

At first, I positioned myself in the wheel house, but soon made my way to the opposite side of the boat and aft to get a better view. The man in charge of the sampan was stoic about this interruption and only warmed up minutes later when he was given two packs of American cigarettes and told the boat's crew was sorry for his inconvenience.

We patrolled far offshore in an area south of the mouth of the bay, an area that was considered not yet secure. Then the Swift boat changed course and headed north to cross the mouth of the bay, inspecting a couple more sampans enroute.

About an hour before we were to return to base, the crew made its planned rendezvous with the larger turbine-powered U. S. Navy picket ship to drop off supplies and mail. After departing the gunboat, higher sea swells began to make the shallow draft Swift boat's ride quite rough. Not being able to make sufficient headway to finish the search track, Barry cut the patrol short and headed back to the protection of the bay.

I didn't know it at the time, but my short and uneventful patrol in the Swift boat was the only time in my twenty-four-year career that I was ever underway with the saltwater Navy. As thrilling as it was to be on the "front lines," it was an alien environment to me. My aviation "sea legs" failed me early on in a vessel that pitched and rolled at the same time. I never got sick but I was always on the verge. To escape any undue attention or razzing from the crew because of my green appearance, I stayed quietly in the background observing and admiring professionals who, in my opinion, were definitely in harm's way more often than those of us who flew above them on patrol.

Chapter 6

NORTH KOREANS SEIZE THE *PUEBLO*

On January 23, 1968, a fleet of North Korean gunboats interrupted Commander Lloyd Bucher's lunch time on board the USS *Pueblo*—and stayed beyond any welcome.

The Navy's intelligence-gathering ship had been quietly drifting nearly sixteen miles off the North Korean coast monitoring communications frequencies in the nearby Wonsan Harbor complex. Then all hell broke loose. First a sub chaser and then three torpedo boats quickly surrounded the *Pueblo* and demanded that it heave to or be fired upon.

Commander Bucher, anticipating intimidation but no action, signaled the uninvited lunch guests that he was in international waters and intended to remain there. Two North Korean MIG aircraft, a fourth torpedo boat and another sub chaser soon joined the fray. Now sensing real danger and being far from any help, he ordered the bridge crew, "Ahead, one third," and to take a course directly away from the coast.

This brave action foiled a North Korean gunboat crew from boarding the *Pueblo* to seize it, but not for long. Though the ship initially made evasive course changes to throw off the pursuers, one of the North Korean sub chasers opened fire with its 57-mm cannon, causing several injuries among the crewmen. Other Korean boats then opened up with their machine guns for several seconds.

Threatened again to "heave to," Bucher responded by ordering full-speed ahead. Then hearing a roar overhead, Bucher saw one of the MIGs fire a warning rocket across the ship that landed two miles ahead. Within a few seconds, all the marauders commenced firing their cannons and machine guns at the ship.

Adding an even greater alarm to the situation, one of the torpedo boats was observed by a *Pueblo* crewman to be uncovering one of its tubes in preparation of firing.

While the ship was being raked with machine gun and cannon fire, a warrant officer aboard the *Pueblo* reportedly took matters into his own hands and stopped the ship by yanking the bridge's engine annunciator to full stop. Conditions went rapidly downhill from there. Now trying to stall for time and continue to burn classified documents, Commander Bucher had faint hopes that some air units would arrive from South Korea or Japan to rescue the situation. Unfortunately, U.S. units were never marshaled in time to thwart the illegal seizure.

With one crewman dying and others seriously wounded, Bucher begrudgingly gave up to avoid additional injuries, deaths, or the total destruction of his ship.

On January 23, I was flying on the first of three Patrol Plane Second Pilot check rides that would lead to my certification as a copilot. My crew and I had repositioned to Sangley Point four days prior and were getting ready to return to Cam Ranh for God, country and Operation "San Magoo." It was not until early in the afternoon the next day that we simultaneously received message traffic on the capture, and could read cursory reports about the *Pueblo* in the Stars and Stripes newspaper.

Though Korea was over 1,700 miles away, we were, nevertheless, incensed—in a detached sort of way—about the brash and aggressive nature of the North Koreans to attack and capture this Navy ship when it assuredly had been in international waters. Like most of the American military in the Far East at the time, we also felt letdown that there had not been a better response to defend or recapture the Pueblo. Echoing that same sentiment about the lack of a forceful response to the capture of the *Pueblo*, the Milwaukee Sentinel newspaper published in an editorial that "Our official bird is not an eagle, hawk or dove. It is a chicken."

As haughty as my crew was in preparing to return to the familiar Market Time patrols, we were caught off guard two days after the *Pueblo* capture by our operations scheduling officer, who informed us he was cancelling our trip back to Cam Ranh.

"Be prepared to leave early tomorrow morning for Iwakuni where you'll work with the Pueblo task force ships being formed in the Sea of Japan."

A carrier strike force with its screening ships was being assembled to confront the North Koreans in the waters near Wonsan Harbor, where the *Pueblo* had been taken. If we had been incensed by the news of the *Pueblo*, now we'd have the opportunity to put our actions where our mouths had been.

We had to dig to the bottom of our foot lockers and duffel bags to find warm enough military and civilian clothing for Japan in the winter. We had packed it, but we didn't believe we'd ever have to use it. Leaving our bathing suits and flip-flops behind, we took off on January 26 for a seven-hour flight direct to Iwakuni. Two other squadrons also sent aircraft to Japan to make up a patrol detachment. Upon landing, crew officers were taken immediately to a briefing to be apprised of the general situation. Returning to our aircraft to pickup our baggage, we were surprised to see our enlisted crew loading live weapons in the bomb bay and rocket pods on the wings. Our hosts hadn't said anything about a conventional war load of weapons at our general briefing.

Loaded for bear

Since joining Patrol Squadron 17 more than a year before, I had never dropped or fired live ordnance. I had fired solid-head rockets for practice and qualifications, and had dropped many blue-colored 100-pound water-sand-filled practice shapes to simulate bombs, torpedoes and mines. Even in Vietnam, except for an occasional M-60 machine gun carried in the aft station for target practice, we went on Market Time patrols unarmed. Now, without any hesitation, our host air wing had ordered all the patrol aircraft to put on full conventional war loads of two Mark 46 torpedoes, three 350-pound contact depth bombs, and twenty-eight rockets in four pods.

All of our previous missions had been passive. Now, for the first time, we were loaded for bear. This Pueblo incident was shaping up to be more of a "war" than Vietnam.

Our first flight, five days after the capture of the *Pueblo*, was a six-hour antisubmarine net in front of the warships in the surface task force cruising through the narrow Korea Strait between Japan and South Korea. In some of the nastiest and roughest weather I had ever flown in up to that time, we dropped floating sonobuoys in several patterns across the strait to monitor acoustically for any submarine threat.

The channelized sonobuoys were activated upon contact with the salt water of the strait and transmitted

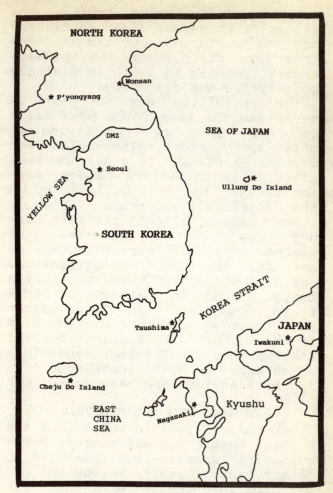

Pueblo operational area

to the aircraft the sounds picked up on the buoys' submerged hydrophones. As bad as the swells were on the surface of the water, we were amused every once in a while to hear the voices of Korean or Japanese fishermen who would see our buoys, haul them into their boats and inadvertently transmit to us their dialogue of surprise and discovery.

The visibility was so poor we never saw the task force pass below us even though we were flying at only 2,000 feet. The cold, wet weather kept us in a deicing mode practically the entire flight, trying to keep ice from building up on the wings, tail and props.

Our second flight the very next day was back in the same foul weather continuing our antisubmarine net for the task force stragglers. Again, while we were monitoring buoys placed in patterns at strategic locations in the narrow strait, we were mostly concerned up in the cockpit with keeping ahead of the weather and icing conditions which made our blind instrument flying both anxious and hazardous.

Armed and dangerous

Our third flight in support of the *Pueblo* task force was another antisubmarine screen, but this time to detect any threats following our warships into the Sea of Japan. The main group had passed through the strait and was assembled off North Korea's Wonsan Harbor, the port where the seized *Pueblo* was located. In order to use our full capability, besides monitoring and analyzing sonobuoy acoustic information, a crewman also monitored the ECM or radar emissions that were in our vicinity. Monitoring ECM could detect a submarine using its radar on the surface to navigate in waters too shallow to safely allow it to run submerged. Tactically, it would not be unusual to see a submarine on the surface in water less than 100 fathoms.

This generally being the case in our area of operation, we had the ECM operator monitor the Soviet radar bands used by their submarines to navigate on the surface. Since both North Korea and China were using Soviet-built submarines and radar, receiving signals in those bands would be cause for us to investigate. In weather that was not much improved from our first two flights, we patrolled the Eastern Channel of the Korea Strait for any submarines attempting to transit undetected. For several hours we had been monitoring buoys and had our radar turned off to help our own ECM search.

"Pilot, this is ECM, I have a medium strength S band contact, bearing one four zero." This ECM call was pretty exciting considering the highlights of our previous days had been Japanese- and Korean-language lessons monitored by us from the buoys "caught" by fishermen.

"I'm coming to a heading of one four zero. Keep me updated, ECM," was the plane commander's reply.

Since I was off the navigation

table and flying in the copilot's seat, the pilot asked the tacco where we were located. He was told we were about 60 miles north of Japan and 60 miles east of the Tsushima Island group. Not wishing to give ourselves away by turning on our own radar until the last moment, the pilot began a slow descent to 1,000 feet and began his run on what he suspected was a Soviet-bloc submarine on the surface or at conning tower level. The "S" band radar, though common to many other Soviet surface vessels, was particular to its surfaced submarines of that era.

We were all pumped up. We knew we "had one cornered." With the signal getting stronger, ECM gave the pilot a small course correction to the source of the radar emission. The pilot then began a gradual descent to 200 feet, hoping he could get below the overcast. Though we were loaded for bear, we did not have a situation which required us to go through our weapons checklist.

Nevertheless, if we found a Soviet or bloc submarine on the surface at the end of our run, we would surely startle the conning tower crew with a low pass and a wing full of rockets.

With the ECM signal getting stronger, we knew we were getting closer to our contact. With the weather remaining cloudy, the pilot thought to ask the tacco where we were in relation to the Japanese coast. As the tacco was beginning to answer, the aircraft came screaming out of a cloud bank at the entrance of a bustling Japanese commercial port, rapidly covering the distance to a dock area where a Soviet freighter was tied up, taking on or off loading cargo. The familiar bright-yellow hammer and sickle on the broad-red band of the smoke stack was a dead giveaway as to the nationality. The rotating horizontal bar next to the stack was our radar emission source.

With an "Oh, shit" for good measure, the pilot made a lazy climbing turn to the right, up and out of the port, I suspect, hoping that no one noticed this low flying armed and dangerous aircraft.

Actually, we never came closer to the freighter than a quarter of a mile and didn't overfly any ships coming in or out of port. As a result of our exciting side trip, we could say one thing for sure: The source of our S band emission did not get away—we definitely had him cornered.

The sealed manila envelopes

With the war of words getting hotter and being waged on a worldwide front between the United States and North Korea over the capture of the *Pueblo*, our last three missions for the task force were long and somewhat mysterious. We were no longer conducting ASW surveillance but surface search between the Korea Strait and South Korea's Ullung Do Island, just 220 miles southeast of Wonsan. North Korea held the crew of the *Pueblo*, and believing it had the bigger propaganda hammer, used exceedingly provocative language. Yet, the U.S. refrained from any military response.

We were still loaded for bear and additionally looking out for Soviet "Bear" patrol aircraft that we had been briefed would be shadowing the task force. Even though the weather had improved, we, again, never did see the task force—or the stalking Soviet reconnaissance aircraft.

One new twist to our last three missions was the sealed manila envelopes we were given that would be opened only if we received a specific coded message over the several frequencies our radio operator was monitoring. To say there was a lot of speculation about the envelopes among crew members was an understatement.

Were we fast enough at our maximum sea level speed of 350 knots to slip into a harbor and sink a ship? We knew we could be accurate in either a rocket or depth bomb attack but we never had to take it beyond conjecture. Surely, if the people in our leadership were going to respond in strength, they would call upon the carrier attack aircraft now deployed with the task force in the Sea of Japan. We never got the signal to open any of the envelopes we carried in the cockpit.

A day after our last mission in the Sea of Japan, a loud "pop" came from our starboard reciprocating engine about twenty minutes after takeoff on our repositioning flight back to the Philippines. A check of the engine analyzer indicated a failure in one of the engine's eighteen cylinders, so a precautionary feathering was accomplished after I got the jet engines back on the line. We had just taken off from Iwakuni heading south and had leveled off at 6,000 feet when the failure occurred. Being heavy with fuel for an anticipated eight-hour flight, and not having a fuel-dumping capability, we had to fly around for two hours to "burn down" to our recommended landing weight before making an uneventful three-engine landing back at Iwakuni. What luck we had having an engine failure at that time rather than in the days just previously.

It took two days for our maintenance crew to remove and replace the damaged cylinder head before we were off again for Sangley Point.

It took eleven months of brutal interrogations, beatings, deprivations and forced confessions before the North Koreans tired of their propaganda exercise and released the eighty-three *Pueblo* survivors and the body of crewman Duane Hodges.

Chapter 7

GUN-RUNNING TRAWLERS

If VP-17 had the misfortune of not detecting any North Vietnamese gun-running trawlers during its 1965-66 and 1966-67 deployments, it more than made up for that deficiency in 1968.

In less than sixteen-days time, squadron crews accounted for the unprecedented detection of four communist trawlers, two of which were subsequently destroyed after battles with surface forces. The skippers of the other remaining trawlers apparently got cold feet or were unsuccessful decoys trying to divert attention to themselves. Nevertheless, the latter trawlers turned tail before crossing the 12-mile territorial boundary, remaining in international waters as they retreated.

VP-17's incredible feat in February 1968 alone accounted for one-third of the twelve steel-hulled enemy gun-running trawlers destroyed, captured or turned back in the three years Market Time had been in operation.

Trawler turns tail

In mid-February, a squadron crew

initially detected a steel-hulled trawler southeast of the Paracel Islands heading in a southerly direction. Market Time headquarters had briefed crews many times that it believed the trawlers were being staged from both the Chinese communist-held Paracel Islands—which were located in the middle of the South China Sea—and Hainan Island, also part of the People's Republic of China.

This trawler was blatantly suspicious. Though built as a 100-foot-long coastal freighter with holds fore and midship, it was rigged with fishing nets, line floats and canvas tarps. The deck was also made to look sloppy, like a typical fishing boat, but the hull and superstructure were in good repair and not rusty like you would expect to find.

This boat was more "fishy" than fishing boat. Moreover, the hull design was exactly the same as all the previous gun-runners, with a large hook-shaped steel plate connecting the lower deck to the pilothouse deck. As in all the past sightings of communist trawlers, this contact was not flying a flag to identify its nationality.

On the lethal side, this trawler had a large canvas tarp draped over most of the raised aft deck behind the pilot house. On nearly all previous trawlers that had been searched after capture, Market Time personnel had discovered 12.7-mm antiaircraft guns mounted and hidden under the aft-deck tarps. Thus, in their attempt to remain covert and not bring attention to themselves while on the open sea, all previous trawlers had refrained from firing at point-blank range on any low-flying reconnaissance aircraft that had passed them on patrol. However, as had been the case, once engaged by seaborne forces, the trawler crews would give up their sham, remove the canvas tarps and use their guns defensively.

Since this first contact was 300 miles east of the South Vietnam coast, the aircrew reported to the Market Time Surveillance Center it had a probable trawler. Then the crew began an over-the-horizon, out-of-sight surveillance of the contact using short radar sweeps every hour to plot the vessel's position. From the series of positions plotted, the crew could calculate the course and speed of the suspect trawler and report that up-to-date information to the control center over a secure (encoded) frequency.

The Market Time center, when apprised it had a probable contact, immediately launched another aircraft to complete the first crew's track. Then the center personnel began predicting where the gun-runner might try to land ashore within the next two days. The VP-17 crew was relieved by another aircraft after eight hours of tracking, and the second crew was relieved eight hours later as the target neared the central coast of Vietnam. In the last stages of the operation, as surface ships were converging on the incoming target, the trawler unexpectedly turned away from the coast for the open sea. Was this a dress rehearsal or a test of the Market Time operation?

Four trawlers make a run

Market Time forces did not have to wait long for more action. For the first time, North Vietnamese planners put together a coordinated attempt to infiltrate hundreds of tons of arms and ammunition into the south on four trawlers. It is only speculation, but the communist planners may have been attempting to overload the Market Time force structure in hope of seeing some limited success.

The enemy set its effort for late February or early March, staging one trawler to make landfall on the north coast, two for the central, and one for the southern-most peninsula of South Vietnam.

By February 29, my crew had been back from the *Pueblo* operation for three weeks and had just completed an additional seventy-three hours of Market Time patrols in ten flights. We were just preparing to start another Market Time preflight when the duty officer approached the plane commander with an urgent request. One of our crews was in contact with a probable trawler and would not be able to complete its track. Incredibly, another one of our crews had made contact with two probable trawlers but had only enough fuel to remain with one of them for a short period of time before returning to Cam Ranh. Could we cut our preflight time to a minimum and takeoff early to intercept the trawler that had not been located for two hours?

"You better believe it!" was the reply. Then the duty officer was off looking to round up another crew as a backup to all this extraordinary enemy activity.

Without compromising safety, we took off one hour early—no time to get coffee from the galley—and flew to a position from which we could talk to our sister crew on the secure radio without being seen by the trawler it was trailing. Since I was flying in the left seat and not on the navigation table, I overheard a time, position, course and speed for the trawler our sister crew had last observed three hours previously.

With this information, our tacco plotted the position and advanced the contact three hours ahead. He then gave me a compass heading to the projected intercept point.

It was about 5 P.M. with an hour to go until dusk when radar called out a target bearing zero six zero at 30 miles. With no other medium-sized radar contacts showing in the area where we expected to find the trawler, I turned directly to the target. Inbound five miles from the target, the plane commander set the crew condition to "rig" or do a visual and photo-identification pass at low altitude.

I saw the target faintly in the waning sun and did a banking turn to the port at 200 feet and 200 knots to parallel the ship's southwesterly course. The plane commander in the copilot's seat called on the internal communications systems for the crew to expect the rig on the starboard side in thirty seconds. Flying parallel and to the left of the foamy wake, we could see we had a classic gun-runner, even down to the hook-shaped deck plating. The ship's crew, of course, could see us and might have felt they could have reached up and touched us as we flew by them. We were that close.

As fate would have it, the captain of the trawler chose not to uncover the canvas tarp he had draped on his aft deck and have his crew treat us to some cannon fire. The trawler was continuing its sham, hoping to get close enough to the coast to make a high-speed run in the dark.

Considering the sun was soon to set, we chose to make another photo-rig run by the trawler in order to ensure good photographs for our intelligence people. After our nervous second pass—never fly over an enemy position more than once—we retreated about 25 miles to the east where we could be assured the trawler could not see us. Then we turned off all of our exterior lights, including our strobe, climbed to 2,000 feet and dropped a sonobuoy in the water to act as a relatively-fixed point in the ocean. The tacco then asked the radar operator for a bearing and distance to a nearby island to confirm the position of the buoy. For the next six hours we continually flew in a lazy racetrack pattern around this buoy, taking quick radar sweeps of the trawler once or twice an hour. The line of plotted fixes indicated the trawler had changed its course and was heading directly for the northern coast of South Vietnam.

About 11:30 P.M. we were relieved by another squadron aircraft that later passed the trawler off to two warships waiting to pounce on the prey. Everything went so well for us on this mission, we all felt elated on our trip back to Cam Ranh. We had to divert farther to the east instead of flying directly to the base to avoid overflying the operation taking place south of us on one of the trawlers trying to infiltrate the central coast.

Our debrief was sketchy, at best, but we learned two of our crews had accounted for the initial discovery of three trawlers, and a sister squadron had detected a fourth trawler south of the mouth of the Mekong Delta. The trawler we had relocated and tracked was the northern trawler, first detected by the crew that had found two enemy vessels but had only enough fuel left to stay with one. We also learned that same crew had stayed on station even longer than it might have been prudent to make a successful hand-off with another aircraft and landed with very little reserve fuel in its tanks.

Since my crew slept through most of the next day and flew back to back flights for the next four days, we didn't learn much from our own people about the outcome of the mass infiltration attempt. We were lucky, however, to pick up a copy of the March 2, 1968 Stars and Stripes newspaper which gave the following account:

*SALVAGE CREWS GET GUNS,
SUPPLIES FROM RED BOATS*

SAIGON (AP) - Salvage crews recovered large hauls of weapons and munitions and 14 enemy bodies Saturday from the three Communist trawlers destroyed Friday in a coordinated gun-running attempt along the coast of South Vietnam.

The three 100-foot trawlers, along with a fourth which was turned away, were first detected two days ago by U.S. patrol planes. They were tracked until they crossed the 12-mile limit into South Vietnamese waters and then engaged by U.S. and South Vietnamese naval units.

"There is no doubt that it was a coordinated and well planned effort," a U.S. Navy spokesman said.

" We now know that all the trawlers were scheduled to make landfall at 1 A.M. on March 1 (Friday). This was their first coordinated effort to infiltrate by sea."

The naval actions brought to 12 the number of enemy gun-running trawlers destroyed, captured or turned back in the three years since allied coastal surveillance began in a campaign known as "Operation Market Time."

One of the three trawlers was forced onto the beach 40 miles south of Chu Lai and blown up by her own crew to avoid capture. The Navy said salvage crews recovered 600 carbine rifles, 41 submachine guns, 11 light machine guns and an assortment of hand grenades, rifle grenades, mortar rounds and other ammunition.

Salvage divers also recovered some weapons from a trawler which exploded during a gun duel with American and Vietnamese naval vessels in a cove 10 miles north of Nha Trang on the central coast. So far, the Navy said, divers have recovered 36 grenade launchers, and 22 AK-47 automatic assault rifles. Bodies of 14 enemy dead were found on the beach or in the trawler hulk, the Navy said.

The third trawler sank in 25 feet of water in the mouth of the Bo De River, 155 miles southwest of Saigon off the Ca Mau peninsula in the southern tip of the country. It exploded in a gun battle with U.S. Navy and Coast Guard ships. Salvage operations were underway Saturday but there was no report so far on recovery of munitions and weapons.

Most of the weapons recovered were of Chinese or Russian make. U.S. Navy spokesmen said the origin of the trawlers had not yet been determined. There was speculation they came from China's Hainan Island on the east side of the Tonkin Gulf. The vessels bore no markings and flew no flags."

It amazed us that we learned more about the overall success of the February 29-March 1 Market Time operation from the newspapers than we did from our own briefing officers.

Chapter 8

P2V SPECIAL OPS IN VIETNAM

From patrol aircraft far out over the South China Sea to the Navy and Coast Guard picket ships and Swift boats that stopped and searched vessels in the coastal areas, Operation Market Time was highly successful in nipping the flow of arms and ammunition into South Vietnam by sea.

Testifying to that success, General Westmoreland, the top U.S. commander in Vietnam, said that after only two years of operation, Market Time had reduced the seaborne flow of arms to South Vietnam from seventy percent to "not more than ten percent."

Unfortunately, the success of Market Time did not slow down the North Vietnamese and Viet Cong for very long. It merely forced them to shift their efforts to the Ho Chi Minh trail system to make up for the seaborne arms losses.

When it became apparent to the American leadership that the north had significantly increased its war material deliveries over the trail system, two Navy squadrons flying highly-modified Neptune models were quickly formed to interdict the expanded supply route. At the same time, the U.S. Army also modified several P2Vs to operate as airborne electronics and communications platforms in the war zone.

VO-67: The green machines

The first combat Neptunes to operate in Southeast Asia were the OP-2E modifications flown by the Navy crews of the quickly-organized Observation Squadron 67 (VO-67). In its short sixteen-month history as a commissioned squadron, this unit was tasked with a critical stop-gap mission that put its aircrews in harm's way on just about every sortie.

I got to see some of the squadron's twelve unique jungle-green aircraft as they were being further modified for their combat mission at Sangley Point. I also later ran into a former VP-17 pilot who was a bombardier/pilot in the unit. Having a few missions under his belt at that time, the most he would say was that every mission was "a very bumpy ride" due to the constant antiaircraft fire from the ground.

In 1967 and 1968 we had an inkling of what the squadron was trying to accomplish. Today, we know more of the story and can acknowledge the courage it took for those crews to fly each day along the heavily-defended roads that made up the infamous Ho Chi Minh trail system.

The increased traffic of arms and ammunition making its way into South Vietnam through Laos after mid-1966 alarmed American strategists. Thus,

Robert S. McNamara, President Lyndon Johnson's secretary of defense, ordered the Army to study the situation and advance a plan to stop the flow. At that time, the destruction of supplies on the Ho Chi Minh trail was being hampered by a lack of intelligence to pinpoint viable targets for the U.S. warplanes flying overhead. Most target acquisitions were being made visually by FAC's (Forward Air Controllers) flying light aircraft at altitude. A better system of determining supply concentrations was needed.

The Army responded to McNamara's challenge by proposing a new method to target trucks and troops passing by acoustic and seismic sensors dropped on the enemy's roads by Air Force F-4 Phantoms. The sensors would be "real time," providing current rather than old intelligence. The U.S. leadership accepted the plan, but got the Navy involved to begin the initial sensor drops because the Army stated it needed twelve months to develop its own proposal. Moreover, the Navy's back was up against a wall when McNamara insisted an operational unit be on line to accomplish the mission by November 15, 1967.

VO-67 was the outgrowth of the Navy's best effort to meet both the Army's plan and McNamara's challenge. But what kind of aircraft already in the inventory could be quickly converted to deliver sensors with pinpoint accuracy? Before any personnel were assigned, the Navy would have to decide what aircraft could fulfill the Army's mission specifications.

The P2V was chosen for several reasons. It had a system in place to deposit sensors—albeit it would have to be changed from ocean sonobuoys to land sensors. Many senior personnel were already familiar with the aircraft and would need only minimal training to modify their experience for the new mission requirements. The dozen SP-2E basic aircraft for the operation were in mothballs and could be readily acquired and remodeled into the OP-2E green machines.

VO-67 was commissioned on February 15, 1967 with less than two-dozen officers and enlisted on hand for the ceremony. The new squadron was spooling up so fast that most other personnel were still in refresher or initial training with the RAG squadron in San Diego or at the SERE survival school when the unit was commissioned.

The aircraft the squadron would soon fly in combat went through their major modification work at the Martin Aircraft company in Baltimore, Maryland. The basic model's large belly radome, wing tip tanks and Magnetic Anomaly Detection (MAD) tail boom were all removed. The two most distinctive features added to the stripped airframe were chaff dispensers in the blunt tail left by the removal of the MAD boom, and the small chin radar below and just behind the bow observer's plexiglas nose. Other equipment added included an aft-fuselage-mounted camera, and a gun-pod stub on the inboard weapons station of each wing.

On the inside of the aircraft, most of the earlier ASW gear was removed for weight considerations except that equipment slated for sensor deployment. The old canvas and rubber fuel tanks were removed and replaced by self-sealing tanks, a Norden bombsight was added to allow precise sensor deployment, and the aft waist windows were modified to accept the placement of manually-fired M-60 machine guns.

One new modification which later proved to be a maintenance headache was the replacement of the original steel propellers for ones made of fiberglass. Those props were lighter but more susceptible to damage from the war zone's debris-laden runways. By the end of its deployment, VO-67 maintenance crews had to replace eighty percent of the new fiberglass propellers.

Ready or not, VO-67 personnel arrived at the Royal Thai Air Force Base at Nakhon Phanom in November 1967 on the date originally insisted upon by McNamara. With little time to settle in and without all of its aircraft, the squadron, nevertheless, flew it first mission only ten days later. Crews were quite senior, owing to the requirement to find personnel already experienced in the aircraft. My former VP-17 buddy, though a senior lieutenant, was the junior officer in his crew. The squadron commanding officer was a captain, one grade senior to just about all other COs in naval air squadrons, and he had an unprecedented eleven commanders to organize his departments. A "normal" squadron had six commanders.

The first squadron loss occurred on January 11, 1968 when a crew failed to return from a sensor-dropping mission along the trail system. Commander D. A. Olsen, the squadron's executive officer, had been assigned the mission that day and had an additional crew of eight on board. Two weeks later, the wreckage of the aircraft was spotted at the base of a cliff where it presumably had crashed while climbing out in poor visibility.

Only two weeks after the last of the squadron aircraft had arrived in Thailand from the Philippines, the unit's second loss was reported. On February 17, a crew flying at 500 feet to drop sensors along the jungle roads was hit by antiaircraft fire. The green Neptune sustained extensive battle damage that included a fire in the starboard recip engine. The VO-67 pilot reported to the F-4 Phantom jet pilots who were escorting his mission that he had sustained damage and that he was climbing into a high cloud bank before changing course for home base.

Several minutes later, a FAC pilot in a light aircraft orbiting above the mission area observed a burning wreckage in the jungle along the Neptune's presumed course to Nakhon Phanom. There were no survivors among the nine crewmen on board.

Ten days later, a VO-67 aircraft dropping sensors on the trail system over Laos was hit by antiaircraft fire that killed one crewman instantly and filled the fuselage with fire and smoke. Having gained some experience from the previous squadron losses, the aircraft commander ordered his remaining crew to bail out before the damaged Neptune became uncontrollable. All of the surviving members of the crew bailed out and seven were rescued by a helicopter in the vicinity. The aircraft commander, however, one of the last to jump, was never found.

Other squadron Neptunes were taking battle damage during their missions but making it back to Thailand intact. Nevertheless, the fatalities and aircraft losses that had occurred due to concentrated antiaircraft fire were unacceptable and needed to be addressed. A conference called to review VO-67's battle-damage statistics recommended minimum-weather conditions over the mission area, alternative assignments and the limitation of one flying pass over the assigned area.

Conferees also suggested that the use of smoke markers by the overhead FAC aircraft be abated if the target was visible to the Neptune crews.

VO-67 continued operations through June 1968 without any more fatalities, anticipating the Air Force would soon be ready to take on the mission to deploy the sensors. The short-lived squadron was decommissioned on the first of July having fulfilled an incredibly-tough mission requirement in very little time.

VO-67 was the only Navy Neptune squadron in the Vietnam theater of operations to sustain flight deaths. Unlike their patrol brethren flying in Neptunes, VO-67 crews, no doubt, faced "thousands of hours of sheer terror, punctuated by moments of boredom."

VAH-21: Trail interdiction

In late 1967, a unique gray-camouflaged Neptune appeared on the ramp at NAF Cam Ranh Bay--and no one was talking. We were told to stay away from the aircraft and not to take photographs . . . but that just whetted our curiosity. We'd just have to buy someone a beer or trade some of our precious "San Magoo" for information.

The four Project TRIM (Trail and Road Interdiction, Multisensor) aircraft were modified from SP-2Hs, the same basic model we were flying in VP-17. The giveaway was the unique-bulged cockpit canopy that was readily recognizable—but everything else looked different. This new Neptune had a different stinger in its tail. In place of the removed

MAD tail boom, the gray aircraft had an awesome twin 20-mm cannon turret that used a night-vision scope for target acquisition. The camo-gray aircraft were also modified with a smaller APQ-92 radar in a pod underneath and forward of the bomb bay doors, where the huge APS-20 radar dome had been installed. Some of the aircraft also had large chin-mounted fairings that housed Low Light Level Televisions (LLLTV), forward-looking infrared sets, and real-time infrared scopes.

In an attempt to suppress the jet-engine noise during combat operations, some of the aircraft were fitted with what looked like hollow fifty-five-gallon steel drums mounted aft of each jet engine exhaust.

Redesignated as the AP-2H, the aircraft was originally modified as a test bed for the Naval Air Test Center to evaluate sophisticated equipment under combat conditions. When the initial evaluation was completed and the right mix of equipment was chosen, the project was redesignated as Navy Heavy Attack Squadron 21 (VAH-21). It continued to operate from Cam Ranh.

The crews did not talk a lot, but one thing I remember from walking by these aircraft just about everyday was the black-powder burns on the 7.62-mm mini gun pods mounted under each wing. Wherever these aircraft and crews were going at night or during inclement weather, they were obviously firing upon enemy targets.

After the Vietnam Conflict was over, I learned much more about VAH-21's operations. An aircraft modeling magazine in late 1974 had a short but enlightening article on both the squadron's unique aircraft and its mission. Beyond what I could ascertain by looking at the aircraft and getting very little information from the crews, the magazine article indicated the AP-2H was installed with Side-Looking A/B Radar (SLAR), an Airborne Moving Target Indicator (AMTI) system, Digital Integrated Attack and Navigation Equipment (DIANE) and "Black Crow" radio energy sensors.

All of this equipment was tested in the war zone for advanced multi-sensor night attack and electronic search and acquisition. The success of the initial evaluation program resulted in much of the equipment being installed in subsequent models of the Navy's A-6 Intruder all-weather attack aircraft.

To put their electronic test beds through combat conditions, the "Road Runners," as the TRIM project personnel called themselves, flew some missions similar to those of VO-67. Flying from Cam Ranh, crews were tasked to drop sensors along portions of the Ho Chi Minh Trail. However, unlike their contemporaries in the green machines, the new mission also attacked ground targets with general purpose incendiary and napalm bombs. The aircraft also had a 40-mm grenade launcher mounted in and shooting out of ports in the closed bomb bay doors, two wing-mounted mini guns and twin 20-mm cannons in the tail.

The crews were so proficient at delivering incendiaries on their targets, they nicknamed one of their combat aircraft "Napalm Nellie."

The TRIM and later VAH-21 operations out of Cam Ranh Bay went on from November 1967 to June 1969. In that time, the most effective weapon evaluated on the AP-2H was the tail cannons, because the gunner could visually correct and walk his bursts of high-explosive incendiary or straight incendiary rounds to the primary target after passing over it. At the low attack altitudes, this human factor oftentimes outscored the automatic bombing system.

According to the 1974 magazine article, most of the missions were flown in the Mekong Delta area, around the hotbeds of enemy activity in the Parrot's Beak zone near Saigon, and in the I and II Corps regions of South Vietnam.

From mission markers painted on the sides of the aircraft, each AP-2H carried crews safely on approximately sixty-five sorties in the war zone before being withdrawn.

The Army's Crazy Cats

When I first arrived at Cam Ranh Bay in November 1967, our Neptunes were in the company of older siblings that had been operating from the ramp at the Naval Air Facility since July. The U. S. Army's 1st Radio Research Company (RRC) were flying modified SP-2Es in new hybrids redesignated as AP-2Es and RP-2Es.

Nicknamed "Crazy Cats," the 1st RRC conducted covert intelligence-gathering operations in all areas of the war zone in Southeast Asia. Since specifics of the unit's missions are still shrouded, the outward appearance of the squadron's aircraft lead me to believe that the AP-2E's primary mission was to monitor enemy-radio communications.

The unit's other aircraft, the RP-2E, was highly modified from its SP-2E beginnings, with the radar and ECM domes removed, a solid nose fairing installed and the addition of, at least, nine fixed antennas. The larger wing tip fuel tanks from the standard SP-2Es were also deleted for smaller, more aerodynamic tip tanks. This aircraft, most likely, was used as a forward-area communications relay, and possibly for some electronic surveillance.

Chapter 9

LOW ALTITUDE AND HIGH JINKS

In May 1968, VP-17 headed home to Whidbey Island after completing its most successful combat-support deployment in Vietnam, to date. The squadron morale was extremely high and all the flight crews looked forward to a lazy eastbound trip across the wide and warm Pacific to arrive at Whidbey Island with perfect timing just as summer was about to begin.

That deployment was the last for me and my squadron mates in our SP-2H Neptunes since our unit had been notified it would begin transition training to the newer P-3A Orion turboprop aircraft in six months. Four months before we made that transition, I was designated a patrol plane commander in the Neptune, something I really considered a personal milestone.

After training in the new aircraft, I returned to Market Time operations in Vietnam in August 1969 for the last time as a P-3 plane commander. Yet, this would not be the last time I would fly in P2Vs. When I left VP-17 and active duty in January 1970, I immediately joined the Naval Air Reserve where I remained for the next eighteen years, alternately flying the SP-2H and P-3A aircraft with VP-71, VP-91 and VP-69.

But back to May 1968 and VP-17's triumphant return home across the Pacific. Our flight from Sangley Point in the Philippines to Guam and subsequently Wake Island was routine and enjoyable. Now being a designated copilot, I no longer had to sit on the navigation table for any of the flight legs, but instead busied myself with flight-plan filing, aircraft loading and the weather.

We arrived at Wake Island in the mid-afternoon under sunny skies, one Neptune landing every twenty minutes until all eleven aircraft were parked on the ramp. Upon landing, we were informed by the squadron "skipper" or commanding officer, who had been in the lead aircraft, that we would have minimum crew rest in anticipation of taking off in the early morning hours for Hawaii. We weren't terribly fatigued, so the minimum crew rest would get us out of Wake sooner and give us two days instead of just one in Hawaii to lay in the sun and relax.

It all seemed like a good idea to us, but little did we know that one of Neptune's deity cronies was scheduling a light and carnival show for us that we would never forget in our lifetimes.

Wrestling with Saint Elmo

It was going to be a dark and

stormy night. No kidding. That's what the Air Force weather forecaster at Wake Island told us. Knowing the low altitudes we had to fly in the unpressurized P2V, the sergeant questioned whether we really wanted to go through those turbulent storm fronts he had forecast on his charts, all incredibly situated on our projected route from Wake to Barbers Point, Hawaii.

He had predicted hundreds of miles of huge cumulonimbus buildups along our course, lightning, moderate to severe turbulence and strong headwinds, all which would reduce the endurance of our twelve-hour flight. Even with all of this reality in our faces, the skipper gave the order to stagger the takeoffs twenty minutes apart for the eastbound flight.

Since Wake was a major Air Force fueling and rest stop along the route to Southeast Asia, the island was teeming with Air Force personnel and flight crews. Thus, while we were filing our flight plan in the operations building, we were approached by an Air Force navigator who had missed an earlier connection. He was hoping to hitch a ride with us to Hawaii. Despite the fact we told him it would take twelve hours, he still pleaded with the plane commander to get on board. He must have figured "a bird in hand . . .," and the P2V had wings.

My turn for the takeoff and subsequent landing was up that night, so I climbed into the left or primary pilot's seat for the flight. With a "full bag of fuel" on board but no ordnance and less than a full complement of crew, we took off at a little less than our 81,500 pound maximum weight into a picture-book starry night. That idyllic situation lasted about thirty minutes, or the time it took us to climb to our 7,000-foot cruising altitude.

From our cockpit vantage point we could see lightning flashes to the east. Then high ominous clouds slowly began obscuring the cheery stars that had been lighting our way.

"Pilot to radar, bring your scope on line. We've got thunder bumpers on our nose," were my first words once we got leveled off and leaned out the engines for long range cruise. My thoughts were to look for possible course changes to weave our way through the less-dense areas of the thunderstorms that were in front of us.

Radar announced there were no holes in the stone wall of storms that were now fifty miles ahead.

"The front on our nose looks pretty solid, pilot. I don't see any obvious direction to go around it or through it," he said. So we stayed on course.

Long before we entered the actual buildups, a condition occurred to us that I had never experienced before or have since. It started with an unreal whirling, whining and crackling sound in our headsets caused by highly-charged static electricity in the air that overpowered our shorter range VHF and long range HF radios. Since our switches were "on" to monitor those radio frequencies, the charged atmosphere in the vicinity of the thunderstorms created a modulating, eerie noise that only Hollywood could otherwise produce for a scary movie.

Then the light show began. White clouds swirled around and enclosed us so tightly that our aircraft was accentuated by its own fuselage lighting. Our bright spinning anti-collision beacon was so distracting, we had to turn it off.

Then we started to glow. If its never happened to you, its hard to explain the surreal glow of St. Elmo's fire as it attaches itself to all the outside surfaces of the aircraft, dancing to and fro in holographic wisps and rolling balls of blue and pink static electricity. Our sniffer scoop on the nose of the aircraft just in front of the pilot's and copilot's wind screens was a particular focal point for a ghostly rolling ball of phosphorescent fire on that night. It would build up rapidly on the scoop and then dissipate slowly in the slipstream over our heads before starting the show all over again. We watched in awe this ongoing carnival show of glowing wings and mesmerizing rolling balls for about fifteen minutes before our roller coaster ride began.

Close in lightning flashes blinded

us temporarily and diverted our attention from our ghostly show to more serious matters. Radar reported we were within three miles of penetrating our first thunderstorm buildups, so the word went out over the intercommunications system for everyone to take their seats or ditching stations and strap in.

The intensity of the updrafts and downdrafts that followed our numerous penetrations of storm cells, intermingled with so many close lightning flashes, was the roughest ride of my aviation career. We were not prepared for the violent initial surge of our first updraft, though I had luckily turned off the autopilot and was flying the aircraft manually. Without warning, our nose pitched up with a shudder at a thirty to forty degree angle. Instinctively, like a survival reaction, both of us in the cockpit were on the yoke trying to push it over, at least, to the neutral position.

Though the fear in our brains screamed at us to push the nose over even more, all of our training kept us from overcorrecting the nose attitude and possibly stalling the aircraft. Beads of sweat began to form on my forehead, but it wasn't because of the heat.

Though we had inadvertently gained more than 700 feet of altitude in just a few seconds, we did not feel rushed to regain our original altitude too quickly—and that was just as well.

A forceful downdraft caught us seconds after we had sufficiently gained control and switched our recip engines from a lean long-range cruise setting to a safer full-rich fuel and higher power setting. We now were descending rapidly with both of us, again, on the yoke, this time trying to pull it back just enough to stop the rate of descent.

When we gained control again, we had dropped 900 feet, or 200 feet below our originally-assigned altitude—and happy to be level at any altitude. But the ride was not over.

We went through about an hour of pumping iron on the yoke, trying to keep our aircraft nose attitude relatively level regardless of our indicated speed or altitude. When the weather eased up somewhat later, we called around the aircraft to see how the crew members had fared. Hopefully, no one was hurt. The aft station observer informed us all his gear had remained secure in the violent turbulence, but that our Air Force passenger had "up-chucked" some of the box lunch he had been wolfishly downing after takeoff.

About five hours into the flight, we were relieved to break out of a storm front into a mixed pink and baby-blue dawning horizon. It was such a relief regardless of the additional seven hours of flying time we had to go before landing in Hawaii. We were rung out but thankful all was well. We had both been on the yoke six or seven times in the previous hours and had brought the aircraft and crew through safely. We also had been able to re-lean the engines for long-range economy cruise in the waning moderate to light turbulence, and were content fuel would not be a problem for the remainder of the flight . . . there weren't too many gas stations out there for a fill up.

When cleared by Honolulu Control to begin our descent from 7,000 feet for the approach into Barbers Point, our port recip engine "popped" when we pulled back the power. While the plane captain checked his electronic engine analyzer and announced to us he thought it was only a slightly-fouled spark plug, the aft station called to ask what the problem was, egged on by our anxious Air Force passenger who had about all he could take for one flight.

After we shut down our engines and the aircrew began unloading their personal gear for the customs and agricultural agents to check, our Air Force passenger paid his final respects to St. Elmo by getting on all fours in front of the crew and kissing the ground. But for us mortal crewmen, it was a different story. Regardless of the fact that he had gotten to Hawaii in one piece and at the time we said he would be there, our passenger did not take the time to thank the crew for the "ride."

Bow pilot: 'I've got it'

The buffoonery that was inherent in human nature on the ground over thousands of years worked its way quickly into the skies once aircraft started to carry more than one person. Most often initiated for comical effect, tricks perpetrated by the more experienced person on the unwary sometimes had fatal consequences . . . but I'm only going to dwell on the fun aspects as I recall them.

I'm sure that each aircraft had its own little nuances that would give the regular personnel some opportunities to play tricks on the uninitiated. Late in my career and flying in the P-3A Orion, one of my enlisted crew members had a midshipman holding on to a rope which was snaked under the door of the aircraft head (bathroom). By making subtle noises in the head and pulling slowly on the rope, he had our academy passenger convinced he had been crawling out inside the wing root with this lifeline tied around his waist to loosen a frozen but pseudo "sphincter valve." Bringing the midshipman to the end of his rope, so that he had to hold on tightly, my crewman then slowly eased up on the tension.

The "middie" was besides himself that he had been given such an important job, being very conscientious and taking in the slack as it was given up. Then creating a great commotion in the head to simulate closing a hatch, the petty officer exited the facility, acting cold, out of breath and fatigued.

Practicing the compassion he would later need as an ensign, the middie sympathized with the jokester by acknowledging he probably had the "shittiest job in the crew."

In the later models of the P2V, the traditional hook for the in-flight jesters was the "bow pilot." The bow observer's seat was "the best seat in the house" and a sought-after location for all in-flight passengers who were not normal crew members. With feet placed on the metal grating and the seat moved forward, the bow station with its clear plexiglas nose cone gave everyone a visual thrill. No matter what the aircraft did, it was visually amplified in the bow station. When the crew did a rigging run on a ship or trawler, the bow station was seven feet closer to the water than the rest of the aircraft. This gave the bow observer an extra tinge of excitement.

Since just about every passenger wanted to eventually sit in the bow station, those in the cockpit usually had to work hard to contain their buffooning natures. Pilots who couldn't contain themselves asked the bow riders if they "would like to fly the aircraft from the bow."

That offer and challenge was usually more than a passenger could pass up. The soon-to-be patsy was told the control handle on the left of the bow seat was a remote autopilot that allowed the bow observer to fly the aircraft to targets that he could see from his position.

In actuality, the black two-axis control handle was a remote searchlight lever that allowed the bow observer to take control of and aim the searchlight. A searchlight azimuth and pitch indicator on the copilot's panel in the cockpit was the link in making this prank work. Once the bow passenger was convinced he could fly the aircraft, he would tell the cockpit, "I've got it."

Then any movements the bow observer made on the searchlight control handle could be seen on the indicator in the cockpit. The aim of this ruse was for the copilot to fly the aircraft based on the movements of the searchlight position indicator, usually going well beyond the deliberate movements of the bow passenger so that the patsy would finally give up and relinquish control in a panic: "You've got it back!"

The more mature flight crews would play with the passenger—with all safety concerns being considered as the highest priority—and let him relinquish control with confidence and depart thinking he had actually been flying the aircraft. This was especially satisfying when someone would be overheard bragging during happy hour at the club that he had flown the venerable Neptune from the bow—and quite well, at that.

'Aircraft on our tail'

Toward the end of my P2V flying days in September 1973 my crew and I were scheduled to participate in a RIMPAC (Rim of the Pacific) exercise with allied forces from New Zealand, Australian and Japan. We were to act as a "blue force" patrol aircraft to locate and track a task force of ships that were attempting to penetrate our territorial waters undetected.

We would be replacing another aircraft on station that had been shadowing the warships hundreds of miles out in the ocean north of Hawaii. We were briefed on tactics, our unique reporting procedure and enemy threats, including the potential to be intercepted by a fighter launched against us from a carrier in the task force.

We took off from Barbers Point in the dark before midnight and made contact with the aircraft we were to relieve. His last known position of the fleet and its projected course proved to be accurate as we popped up to altitude, took a few radar sweeps, plotted the positions of the ships and relayed the information back to base.

In between our random radar sweeps, we would shut down that emitting equipment and snoop the skies passively for our opponent's ECM or radar signals. That information would potentially tell us what type of ship or aircraft our adversaries had deployed.

The mission was going quite smoothly when my venerable ordnance chief, a veteran of World War II who had loaded weapons on Wildcats and Corsairs at Espiritu Santo in the South Pacific, was startled by an approaching light on our tail. I've never had as much of an adrenaline rush as that night when the chief shrieked, "We have an aircraft on our tail. I can see his light!"

A veteran chief rarely shrieks, but when he does, a young pilot takes notice. I spilled coffee all over my right leg in my frantic rush to grab the yoke, switch off the auto pilot and pull off all the power.

Without waiting for amplifying information, I nosed the aircraft over into a steep starboard turn and descended rapidly on a heading opposite to what we had been flying. Once we were established rapidly dropping toward the water, I called back to the chief, asking him if he still could see the interceptor's light in the dark. After a few seconds to orient himself to our new heading, the chief said he believed the aircraft was now a little off our nose but still closing.

Even in this peacetime exercise, I really didn't want to be intercepted by the task force CAP (Carrier Air Patrol) and become a simulated shoot-down statistic. So, my best bet was to turn off all of my exterior navigation lights and head as low as I dared go over the choppy ocean where a fighter's radar return might be degraded. I continued a rapid descent to 500 and then a shallower cruise to 200 feet above the waves. I asked ECM if he had intercepted any airborne target acquisition radar. He said he had not.

Now with a need to orient myself to the location of the interceptor, I asked the chief if he still saw the aircraft. There was a long silence.

"I guess I just need a new eyeglass prescription, Mr. McGuiness. It was just a bright star on our tail," replied the chief.

Four hours later as we cruised at altitude, some 100 miles from the task force and only ten minutes to the end of the exercise, the chief called to report another visual contact—a real one this time. In the dawning light, he observed a U.S. Navy twin-engine S-2 "Stoof" approaching us on our port-aft quarter. We had not been earlier apprised of this contact by either our radar or ECM, but I could see it in the distance over my left shoulder.

When the S-2 was within about three miles, I asked the copilot to get the jets on the line. When the jets were up and operating, I began a steep climbing turn to the left, quickly rising several thousand feet above the Stoof. After the aircraft passed underneath, I had the jets brought back to idle and pulled the power back on the recips to descend to a level tail position behind the S-2. A short but poignant simulated-verbal burst of machine gun fire, "Ta, ta, ta, ta, ta, ta. . .." over the guard radio frequency let the S-2 pilots known where we were.

Moon under Honolulu

At the end of the RIMPAC exercise, where we had been intercepted by a star and a Stoof, the entire crew fought to keep awake as the rising sun glared fiercely in our faces. We were on our way back to Barbers Point to debrief our flight and then hopefully to get some sleep.

I didn't want it to happen, but I tried so hard to overcome the fatigue and buzz in my head that I caught my third wind and couldn't let it go. The same thing happened to several on the crew—they were so tired, yet, they couldn't sleep.

Somewhere in this foggy state, one of the crew members who had rented a car suggested we go downtown to Honolulu, only thirty-minutes away, have a few drinks, get a little sun and then return to the base to sleep a little prior to dinner.

About six of us bought into this hare-brained adventure and proceeded after showering to begin liberty on hotel row in the downtown area. It wasn't exactly an exciting place to be, since most people were just getting out of bed at 10 A.M. and having leisurely breakfasts on their lanais. Not so surprisingly, we ended up at an underground bar where the sun would not be so challenging to our sensitive eyes. When our vision adjusted to the darkness, we realized by the curved anatomy cruising by behind the bartender that we were observing swimmers from an underwater picture-window-sized viewing port.

An Aussie couple sitting at the bar, who by the nature of their loud conversation might have been there for quite some time, were making running commentaries on the aquanauts making strokes by the large viewing port.

"Now there's a nice one, Luv," said the male gawker, as a bikini-clad wahini swam slowly and sensuously by the glass.

It wasn't long before a little tyke holding on to the pool side averted everyone's attention in the bar by slipping down his trunks to expose himself in a silent ritual explicit of a youth having too much fun for any side trips.

Not to miss an opportunity, the lady announced to all who might be eavesdropping, "Oh look, Steven, it's as big as yours."

As opportunities come and go, I got a tap on my shoulder from Chief Bobbie who must have had a desire to entertain that day. With a sleep-deprived glaze in his eyes and amusement on his brain, he whispered he could "do better" than our most recent screen test and went off with a big smile on his face.

It was about the time we got our second round of drinks when a great white whale of a man dog-paddled by the bar viewing port, all the while searching with his hands for the outline of the window in the south end of the pool.

Though we never saw his face, the chalk color of his skin was a dead giveaway for a middle-aged Northwest sailor who hadn't gotten any sun prior to this duty in the tropics. This white species of whale was unlike the subject of Herman Melville's novel, *Moby Dick*. After some flailing about to stabilize himself in the water, our compatriot executed a precise maneuver with military precision, to give all in the bar a royal Hawaiian Moby Moon to remember.

Unbelievably, the chatterbox Aussie lady at the bar, who was closest to the action, was speechless this time. Glancing over his shoulder, the bartender, no doubt, a veteran of many such exposures, shook his head and rolled his eyes unapprovingly.

Our assembled crew, on the other hand, raised our glasses and our voices in a chorus to give the chief a hearty "ten" for his olympic performance.

Chapter 10

NEPTUNE REIGNS

Eight Neptune variants

I had the luck to be a patrol plane commander in the last Lockheed production-model Neptune, but many variants came before my time that surely deserve recognition. To begin explaining Neptune's long reign, we have to go back to World War II when a Lockheed-subsidiary design team saw the need for a bigger, more powerful land-based patrol aircraft to replace the company's patrol aircraft that had been modified from commercial airframes.

Concept and prototypes: Slated to be built from the ground up for the purpose, the Lockheed Company formally commenced work on the new patrol bomber in December 1941. Unfortunately, America's forced entry into World War II that same month put the design and preliminary work on the back shelf. It wasn't until early 1944 when the Navy resurrected the project and ordered two prototypes and fifteen first-run production models.

Designated the Model 26 design,

Lockheed had the first prototype, the XP2V-1, flying only thirteen months after the initial order. It was May 17, 1945, just three months before the end of war, when the tricycle geared, streamlined aircraft made its way into the air. Named Neptune for ancient Rome's mythological god of the sea, the two prototypes and first subsequent production models appropriately had "Roman" or curved nose assemblies.

The prototype additionally included a mid-fuselage-mounted wing, a high vertical stabilizer, two Wright Cyclone R-3350-8 reciprocating engines and six .50-caliber machine guns in twin-nose, dorsal and tail housings.

The first model could carry combinations of weapons in its bomb bay to a maximum of eight-thousand pounds. The prototype was not pressurized, as were all subsequent P2V variants, but it carried oxygen to allow the crew to attain a service ceiling of up to 22,000 feet for operational necessities. From an aviator's perspective, a unique feature of the aircraft was a hydraulically-actuated varicam, an elevator trim panel attached to the horizontal stabilizer which gave either pilot a mechanical advantage when the aircraft was in a nose-heavy or tail-heavy trim condition.

The new Lockheed patrol bomber also performed well by exceeding the company's Ventura and Harpoon models in operational ranges by over 2,200 statute miles, all without sacrificing maximum speed.

The two prototypes were tested over a thirteen-month period before being delivered to the Navy in July 1946.

P2V-1: Before the end of prototype testing, production began on the fifteen P2V-1s that had been ordered earlier by the Navy. The first of these aircraft became the highly-modified, record-breaking "Truculent Turtle." Otherwise, this production model was not much different from the prototypes except for a larger, permanent radome mounted on the bottom of the fuselage, forward of the bomb bay doors; and a prominent strut-mounted, teardrop-shaped ECM antenna, forward of the astrodome hatch.

In March 1947, the first squadron to receive P2V-1s was the U.S. Navy's VP-ML-2, which was based in California. The new aircraft had been designed for a crew of eight personnel. The pilots found the new aircraft smooth and responsive to fly. The cockpit crew was especially pleased with the Neptune's high rate of climb and its single-engine flight characteristics during an emergency.

Unlike the problems encountered by The Truculent Turtle on its record-breaking flight, the aircraft delivered to the squadron had wing and tail deicers installed for inclement weather.

P2V-2: This model **Neptune** lost its predecessor's Roman nose with its twin .50-caliber machine guns for a longer streamlined solid nose housing six forward-firing 20-mm cannon. The P2V-2 also was visually unique with its "hump back" dorsal fairing mounted between the cockpit and the astrodome. Some aircraft also had a prototype search radar housed in an aft ventral installation in addition to a small standard radome forward of the bomb bay doors.

The new Neptune was produced with more powerful R-3350-24W engines, generally with three-bladed Hamilton Standard propellers. To give even more takeoff power when required, the airframe was also modified for eight JATO stations, four on each side.

All of the models would retain the twin .50-caliber machine guns in the dorsal turret, but after the ninth of eighty-one aircraft produced, the Navy replaced the twin .50-caliber tail turret with a pair of 20-mm flexible cannon. More offensive firepower was added with the installation of sixteen wing stations for five-inch rockets, eight under each wing. Though crew requirements were reduced to seven personnel, the range of the new aircraft was somewhat reduced by the addition of the new equipment and armaments.

Two aircraft in this model were modified as P2V-2Ns to accommodate skis for snow and ice landings during Operation Deep Freeze, the study and aerial exploration of the Arctic region.

P2V-3: This truly ubiquitous model of the Neptune carried out ground-attack and bombing missions in Korea, proved itself as a long-range nuclear bomber that could takeoff from an aircraft carrier, transported VIP personnel into combat areas, acted as an early warning radar platform and performed its normal surface and ASW patrols.

Lockheed produced eighty-three of these Neptunes in the various mission configurations and delivered them to the Navy from August 1948 through January 1950. All of the dash-three variants had the newer, more powerful, R-3350-26W reciprocating engines that could provide 3,200 horsepower for several minutes during takeoff with the selectable addition of water/alcohol injection to the carburetors.

Some variants of the dash-three retained the dash-two's distinctive hump back fairing, reported to be an ECM antenna housing that could detect enemy radars.

Patrol crews already based in the Far East and flying the new P2V-3s were called upon to perform extraordinary ground-attack missions early in the Korean War. The war, which began in June 1950 with the invasion of the south by the north, caught the American leadership unprepared. The first American ground troops sent into action were not fully supported and, therefore, aviation units already on the scene had to be mustered for sorties potentially outside their normal mission profiles.

Neptunes in the war zone performed strafing, rocket, bombing and photographic intelligence missions for a brief period in the beginning of the conflict before being relieved by regular attack squadrons.

The Navy's need for a long-range nuclear bomber was the basis for the P2V-3C variant. To be launched from the deck of a fast carrier, the aircraft was to penetrate deep into enemy territory, deliver its weapons and return to a friendly land base or ditch alongside the launch ship. To accomplish this mission, the basic dash-three model was stripped of its fuselage radome, astrodome, dorsal turret and fixed nose cannon, wing rocket stubs and tail skid. Additional fuel tanks were installed in the nose—just behind a small radar dish—and in the aft fuselage areas. The only defensive weapon kept from the basic model was the twin 20-mm tail cannon.

The long range Neptune bomber concept was proven in March 1949 when a P2V-3C took off from the carrier USS *Coral Sea* on a free deck launch aided by JATO. The aircraft was at a record weight of 74,000 pounds, carried a huge five-ton dummy-weapons load, yet flew nonstop from the Atlantic Ocean to a west coast target area and back to a base in Maryland.

The P2V-3W aircraft came on the scene in mid-1949 to incorporate the APS-20 search radar, one of the best and most reliable systems the Navy had in its inventory through the 1970s. The sizeable-dish antenna of the new system required a larger than standard radome installation between the nose wheel well and bomb bay doors. As an early warning radar aircraft, the variant proved itself in both fleet operations and coastal patrols.

The sixteen P2V-3B low-level radar bombing aircraft produced were modified from other existing P2V-3 variants. Most of these aircraft utilized the ASB-1 special armament system, the same installed in the A-3 Skywarrior, but a few were used for flight testing of advanced electronics.

Two P2V-3Zs were produced as combat transport aircraft for VIP personnel. Visually, the aircraft lacked nose cannon ports and dorsal turrets. It also could be distinguished by its non-standard four-bladed propellers. Internally, the aircraft fuselage was beefed up with armor plating while providing a higher comfort level for the intended VIP passengers. Owing to the time of their service, both aircraft were involved extensively in Korean War operations and planning.

P2V-4 (P-2D): The dash-four model was the first production Neptune to utilize electronic underwater sound surveillance in its antisubmarine warfare (ASW) mission. Before the addition of expendable sonobuoys and the equipment that monitored the system, Neptune crews had to rely upon happenstance visual sightings or radar targets in order to engage threatening submarines.

The addition of the sonobuoy operator to the P2V-4 crew gave the Navy its first all-weather capability of locating and tracking submarines that were snorkeling or cruising on the surface. The new sonobuoys could be dropped in patterns that would cover wide areas of ocean or straits between land masses where hostile submarines could be expected to transit. Each sonobuoy in the water had a deployed hydrophone extending to a selectable depth beneath it that transmitted the ocean's sound sources to the aircraft. The unique sound energy from a submarine diesel engine or auxiliary equipment used in snorkeling or running on the surface would be picked up on the buoys.

The sub's location could then be fixed by an operator who utilized comparative listening between the buoys. Refined later as "Jezebel," the passive sonobuoy system was a huge advance in the Neptune's ASW mission.

Also increasing the mission potential of the dash-four model was the permanent installation of the APS-20 radar in the entire production line.

Though not all aircraft were initially powered by the more powerful R-3350-30W turbo-compound engines, the entire dash-four fleet of fifty-two airframes eventually had those engines retrofitted to produce 3,750 horsepower for takeoff power, turning four-bladed propellers.

The P2V-4 had the same armament as its predecessor, but looked different due to the addition of under wing tip tanks. The fuel tanks, visually similar to those used in 1946 by "The Truculent Turtle," gave the dash-four an extended total range of 4,200 statute miles.

The dash-four was the first of the Neptune series to be installed with an aerial searchlight that was mounted in a plexiglas cone in the forward part of the starboard under wing tip tank.

In 1962, as the P2V-4s were finishing up their service lives in Naval Reserve units in the United States, they were the first Neptunes redesignated as P-2Ds under a new directive from the Bureau of Navy Weapons.

P2V-5 (P-2E): This model accounted for the largest production in Lockheed's Neptune line. A total of four-hundred twenty-four airframes were produced starting in late 1950, just in time to see operational service in the Korean War. The U.S. Navy, alone, took possession of three-hundred forty-eight of the aircraft. The remaining dash-fives were the first Neptunes to be purchased by foreign allied governments through the MAP (Military Assistance Program). Since the late 1950s and through their useful service lives, dash-five aircraft or variants thereof were operated by the governments of Argentina, Australia, Brazil, the United Kingdom, the Netherlands and Portugal.

The first dash-five model to roll off the line was considerably different than the final version. For the first time, the Neptune was modified from the previous model to contain a twin 20-mm Emerson ball turret in the nose. The model retained its twin .50-caliber dorsal turret and its twin 20-mm tail cannon.

Other than its one flight test model and some other individually modified aircraft, all other dash-fives came off the production line with large wing tip fuel tanks, each containing 350 gallons. The starboard wing tip tank additionally contained a directional searchlight in its forward section, and the port tank contained an APS-8 search radar dish in its nose fairing. All models of the dash-five, except the OP-2Es and RP-2Es, retained the large belly radome that housed the APS-20 search radar dish.

In the pluses and minuses of adding equipment and fuel to an aircraft without increasing horsepower, the dash-five model had a reduced maximum airspeed and a range of 4,050 statute miles, both figures only slightly less than its dash-four predecessor.

Early in the production, some airframes were modified with the installation of a plexiglas observer's nose in place of the 20-mm cannon turret, and with the replacement of the 20-mm cannon tail turret with a distinctive long fiberglass "boom" tail to house the ASW MAD (Magnetic Anomaly Detection) sensing head. The plexiglas nose and MAD boom tail would be the dash-five standard halfway through the total model production. The MAD gear would allow a Neptune flying low over the water to detect a substantial iron object, whether submarine or sunken hulk, with pinpoint accuracy. This could provide a weapons-delivery drop point to destroy an otherwise invisible hostile submarine.

A substantial number of airframes were modified late in the production with the installation of J34-WE-34 turbojet engines in pods and pylons beneath the wings, outboard of the reciprocating engines. These later airframes were designated P2V-5Fs. The Navy called for the jet engines to enhance takeoff power, as a backup for a reciprocating engine failure in flight, and as a means of increasing the aircraft's sprint speed in tactical situations. Four rocket launch stations on each wing had to be removed to accommodate the installation of the jet engines.

The only defensive armament remaining on the dash-five "F" models was the twin .50-caliber machine guns in the dorsal turret.

The P2V-5FD model modification was produced in small numbers to provide target drone launch and control, and target towing. After the removal of all wing rocket stubs and the wing tip tanks, pylons were installed outboard of the turbojet engines to carry and launch target drones. Since this aircraft would only be scheduled for utility missions, the defensive twin .50-caliber dorsal turret was also removed.

The P2V-5FE, with new Julie and Jezebel ASW systems and other improvements, was the test bed for the more numerous P2V-5FSs, better known in the fleet after 1962 under the designation of SP-2E.

The SP-2E's primary mission was advanced ASW. As such, all of the former defensive armament that P2Vs had installed in prior years was deleted. Antisubmarine Neptunes now would primarily be electronic hunters whose weapons would more than likely be ocean depth bombs or torpedoes and to a lesser extent the rockets that were retained on the wings.

The SP-2E would use more brain than brawn to find its prey, a snorkeling or submerged enemy attack or missile-carrying submarine. The stakes were getting higher in the mid-1950s when long-range cruise missiles were being deployed on board submarines. Before Neptune's reign was over in the 1970s, the threat would be even greater, as faster and longer-range ballistic missiles were being installed on Soviet nuclear submarines.

To counter this greater threat, two new ASW systems were installed on the SP-2E models, a vastly improved passive-listening system named Jezebel and an active system called Julie. From a pattern of Jezebel sonobuoys placed in the path of a snorkeling or surfaced submarine, an alert Neptune crew could tract the ship's course. Flying in to further investigate or attack the target submarine, if the sub submerged, the Julie system of active underwater echo ranging could produce a fix that the aircraft could confirm with MAD detection for a depth bomb or torpedo attack. All of the new enhanced sub hunters also had installed an improved ECM system that allowed crews to monitor, analyze and triangulate enemy radars.

The Army's AP-2E and RP-2E variants, and the Navy's OP-2E Vietnam combat models, all were derived from SP-2Es and were reviewed in chapter eight of this book.

P2V-6 (P-2F): In late 1952, the Lockheed Company produced the sixth Neptune variant under the designation of P2V-6. This standard dash-six model was later designated as the P-2F. Of the eighty-three airframes produced, fifty-three went to the Navy to fulfill special mine-laying and missile launching missions. Most of the remaining aircraft were made available to France under the MAP.

The P2V-6 was a formidable aircraft with a longer nose to house an Emerson twin 20-mm cannon ball turret. The fuselage retained the twin .50-caliber dorsal turret configuration and the tail bristled with a twin 20-mm cannon turret. Due to its intended mine laying, high- and low-level bombing, torpedo attack and missile-launching missions in combat areas, the basic model also was installed with over one-thousand pounds of armor plating.

The new dash-six aircraft retained the big wing tip tanks from its predecessor but lost the big APS-20 radome for a smaller belly-mounted fiberglass fairing that housed either the APS-33B or APS-70 radar units.

Of the four dash-six variants, the most significant was the P2V-6M, an airframe modified to carry and launch up to two Fairchild AUM-N-2 Petrel air-to-underwater missiles. These new but short-lived weapons were air-launched anti-shipping torpedoes designed to attack enemy military or cargo vessels from a modest standoff distance.

For about two years in the late 1950s, Patrol Squadrons 17 and 24 were redesignated as heavy mining attack units (VAHM) and equipped with P2V-6Ms to perform mining and Petrel-launch missions.

P2V-7 (P-2H): This was the last Lockheed-built Neptune model. When the last of the three-hundred eleven dash-seven airframes was completed in April 1962, the aircraft company could justifiably be proud of its seventeen-year production line that accounted for one-thousand fifty-one Neptunes in seven models. Yet, the P2V production line would continue in Japan for another seventeen years.

The last Lockheed variants were a lot like their SP-2E predecessors but with more powerful R-3350-32W engines, an improved cockpit canopy and smaller wing tip tanks. The APS-20 radar with its larger radome was also installed but moved forward on the fuselage immediately behind the nose wheel well doors. All of the dash-seven models except the initial order going to Canada through the MAP were fitted on the production line with two J-34-WE-36 turbojet engines.

Later designated the P-2H, the new Neptune was the fastest Lockheed production model of the seven variants, with a maximum operational speed of 350 knots. Because of the additional weight of its improved electronic systems, the 3,700 statute mile range of the aircraft was modestly less than the dash-five model.

Though some early production airframes had defensive armaments, subsequent fuselages deleted all of the former fixed machine guns and cannon in consideration of its primary ASW mission. Even in this defenseless configuration, the superb reputation of the Neptune in the allied world produced many orders for the last production line. Thus, the P-2Hs served with the military forces of Australia, Canada, France, Japan and the Netherlands.

In the early 1950s, the new SP-2H patrol aircraft was the epitome of the United States' technical advancements to confront the growing worldwide Soviet submarine threat. The aircraft contained the most advanced systems available to conduct all-weather ASW operations with a high probability of successful "kills." Though it never came to that, the proven capabilities of the Neptunes, and later the P3V Orions, definitely helped keep the enemies of the United States in check during the Cold War.

The last variant of the Neptune line produced by Lockheed carried the passive Jezebel, ECM, MAD and Sniffer systems, and the active Julie, searchlight, paraflare, and radar systems to enable an experienced crew to fly for long distances, deploy on patrol, locate, track and, if necessary, destroy a threatening submarine. The SP-2H was retired by the active duty Navy in the late

1960s but continued with the Naval Air Reserve for another six to seven years.

Four P2V-7s were modified from the production line with retractable aluminum skis, JATO attachments and larger 350-gallon wing tip tanks. These aircraft, redesignated LP-2Js, operated with VX-6, a Navy squadron that explored and did rescue work in Antarctic during the International Geophysical Year.

Seven P2V-7 airframes were customized for the U.S. Air Force under the designation RB-69A. These distinctive "Black Birds" were reportedly used for CIA electronics and intelligence gathering from the late 1950s through the 1960s. Visually, the aircraft had a clipped MAD tail boom, there were no wing tip fuel tanks, and a side-looking airborne radar was installed on the aft starboard side of the fuselage.

The four AP-2H aircraft modified from P2V-7 airframes and used in Vietnam by VAH-21 are described in chapter eight of this book.

Kawasaki-built Neptunes: The Lockheed Company licensed Kawasaki Industries to build P2V-7 models for the Japanese Maritime Self Defense Force. Under this contract, the Nagoya-based company produced forty-eight airframes.

In 1961, the Japanese military bid out specifications for a future turboprop patrol aircraft. Kawasaki responded with a submission to modify its P2V-7 airframe to meet the proposal. Redesignated the P2V-kai or **P-2J** by Kawasaki, the new aircraft would have General Electric T-64 turboprop engines installed to replace the former R-3350 piston engines and would retain the jet engine pods, though the new jets would come from a Japanese manufacturer. The kai, or eighth and last Neptune-type variant, would also have a smaller radome housing an APS-80 search radar, a longer fuselage forward of the wing root and, a larger vertical stabilizer and rudder. Other changes from the former P2V-7 Neptune model included a more modern dual-wheel main landing gear. With increased power and a lower overall gross weight, the P-2J had a greater operational range than the P2V-7.

The last of eighty-two P-2Js produced by Kawasaki was rolled out of the company's Nagoya hangar in March 1979, ending a thirty-four year Neptune production run.

* * *

It is just a little bit ironic that the last Neptune produced was made in Japan—one of two countries it was originally produced to defeat.

Along with Masdas, Toyotas and Nissans, the final Neptune rolled out must have been a reflection of the vast changes that had occurred in the world situation and the new alliances that had been made since late 1945.

BIBLIOGRAPHY

1. *The Naval Aviator's Guide*
   By U.S. Naval Institute
   Annapolis, Maryland
   1963

2. *In Pursuit of Wings . . .*
   By LCDR Paul N. Mullane
   Naval Aviation News, March 1973
   CNO & NAVAIRSYSCOM
   Arlington, VA

3. Patrol Squadron Seventeen
   June 1950 to January 1969
   Command History copy

4. VP-17 Cruise Book
   November 1967 to May 1968
   Vietnam, Philippines, & Korea

5. Navy Model SP-2H Aircraft
   Natops Flight Manual
   CNO & NAVAIRSYSCOM
   Arlington, VA

6. *The Last of the Neptunes . .*
   Airborne ASW Log, July 1979
   Lockheed Aircraft Corporation
   Lockheed staff

7. Naval Aircraft *NEPTUNE*
   NAVAIRNEWS
   CNO & NAVAIRSYSCOM
   Arlington, VA
   October 1977

8. *Trawler!*
   By CDR Charles R. Stephan USN
   Naval Institute Proceedings
   Annapolis Maryland
   September 1968

9. *Cutters and Sampans*
   Senior Chief D. Noble USCG (Ret)
   Naval Institute Proceedings
   Annapolis, Maryland
   June 1984

10. *Salvage Crews Get Guns,
    Supplies from Red Boats*
    Stars and Stripes Newspaper
    Far East Edition
    March 2, 1968

11. *Navy Plane Down In Gulf of Siam*
    Stars and Stripes Newspaper
    Far East Edition
    April 6, 1968

12. *The Naval Air War in Vietnam*
    Peter Mersky & Norman Polmar
    Nautical and Aviation Pub.
    Annapolis, Maryland
    1981

13. *P2V Neptune in action*
    By Jim Sullivan
    Squadron/Signal Publications
    Carrollton, Tx
    1985

14. *Bucher: My Story*
    By Cdr Lloyd M. Bucher USN
    Dell Publishing Company
    New York, NY
    1970

15. *P-2 Neptune*
    By Walt Fink
    IPMS- Vol 10, No 1
    Fall 1974

16. *Flight Jacket* - 1964 Classes
    U.S. Naval School, Preflight
    Pensacola, FL

To order additonal copies of:

COFFEE ON THE WING BEAM

Paperback edition
@ $11.95 (U.S.) each   _____

Shipping and handling
@ $2.00 (U.S.) for
first and $1 for each
additional book   _____

Washington State
residents add $1.00
(U.S.) each book   _____

      Total: _____

Payment enclosed:
__ Personal check   __ Money order

__ VISA   __ MasterCard

Account # _____
Card expires _____

Signature _____
Today's date _____

Mail this form to:
  Knights of the Red Branch Press
  P.O. Box 296
  Clearlake, WA 98235-0296

Your book will be mailed to:
Name: _____

Address: _____

_____

Allow four-six weeks for delivery.